About the autho

Judi James has been speaking at business
conferences and running corporate training
courses for leading UK companies for seventeen
years. She writes a regular column in *CosmoGirl*
and a weekly body-language feature for the
Mail on Sunday called Body Talk, and has been
frequently consulted as a behavioural expert on
Channel 4's *Big Brother's Little Brother*. Her bestselling books include *BodyTalk, BodyTalk at
Work* and *More Time, Less Stress*.

Other books by the author

BodyTalk
BodyTalk at Work
More Time, Less Stress

sex
signals

decode them and send them

sex
signals

decode them and send them

JUDI JAMES

PIATKUS

Visit the Piatkus website!

Piatkus publishes a wide range of bestselling fiction and non-fiction, including books on health, mind, body & spirit, sex, self-help, cookery, biography and the paranormal.

If you want to:

- read descriptions of our popular titles
- buy our books over the internet
- take advantage of our special offers
- enter our monthly competition
- learn more about your favourite Piatkus authors

VISIT OUR WEBSITE AT: www.piatkus.co.uk

Copyright © 2003 by Judi James

First published in Great Britain in 2003 by
Judy Piatkus (Publishers) Ltd
5 Windmill Street
London W1T 2JA
e-mail: info@piatkus.co.uk

The moral right of the author has been asserted

*A catalogue record for this book is
available from the British Library*

ISBN 0 7499 2413 6

This book has been printed on paper manufactured
with respect for the environment using wood from
managed sustainable resources

Typeset by Action Publishing Technology, Gloucester
Printed and bound in Italy by
Legoprint SpA

Contents

Introduction

Did you know that body language is one of the most powerful influencers in the meeting/dating/mating process?

According to research done by a psychologist, during normal face-to-face conversations the words you use account for as little as 7 per cent of the impact of your overall message. During the meet/date/mate process, though, even that paltry score slumps considerably lower. The impact of your body language signals, however, will be 55 per cent and rising of the total message, giving any interested party a whole raft of information about your self-esteem, emotional baggage, sensuality and sexual preferences. So while your verbal chit-chat might be telling your potential mate one thing, the way you stand, move, gesture and smile might be revealing a completely different message.

When a new partner spots you for the first time, his or her conscious mind may well be assessing you from the way you look, smell and sound, but to be *truly* attractive to them you will need to make an impact with more than mere physical beauty and fashion sense. Because while the superficial pairing and bonding process is under way, his/her subconscious mind is making many vital decisions of its own, striving to decipher your stronger, more powerful sexual signals, and calculate the odds on forming a fruitful sexual, emotional and intellectual match.

The way you hold yourself – together with the overall rhythm of your movements – will send out far more potent signals about compatibility and attraction to a potential mate, then, than mere physical 'perfection', and often in just the first few seconds of meeting. Physical beauty has its role in the calculations, but good looks can be either a turn-on or a turn-*off* if they mean that you are seen as visually incompatible – in other words too far off the scale in either direction for your audience. Good looks may appeal to the eye and the ego, but it's the sensual signals which will truly pluck at the reproductive organs, and the signs of preferred behavioural and emotional style which will finally take control of the heart.

Social attraction factors, then, form only a very small part of what is a complex sexual – and emotional – process. Yet since you were small you have been bombarded with advice on making yourself more alluring to a mate, with the bias from magazines and books tilted heavily towards weight loss, spot-zapping and a lifetime's stroll through the acres of cosmetic and fashion products currently available. Your working role models probably were and indeed still may be movie and pop stars.

However, this pressure on us from childhood both to mimic and be attracted by a global ideal is based on little more than wind and water. We strive to be visually acceptable to attract a partner, despite the fact that the role models we copy, the social ideals – models, musicians and actors – rarely seem, in reality, either to get or keep a date, let alone make long-term happy relationships.

The mating process is complex, and based on individual preference, not a social ideal. For that potential date to find you irresistible, or even succumb to that disease known as love at first sight, you will have to score in terms of at least most – if not all – of the following crucial factors:

1. You will need to be reasonably close on the scale of social physical beauty. Too ugly and you could repel; too stunning and you may be seen as unobtainable.
2. You will need to transmit signals – through your posture, walk and gestures – of matching sensuality, sexual drive and sexual preference.
3. You *may* need to display – through your body movement and shape – appropriate breeding potential.

4. You will need to suggest – again through your facial expressions, gestures and posture – behaviour patterns that are either a familiar match or somehow in keeping with echoes going back into his/her childhood.
5. You may need to display – through clothing, accessories, speech or physical presence – an ability to protect and take care of a partner, either financially, intellectually or through physical strength.

Lipstick, aftershave, hair gel, fashion and dieting can all play their part in the process, but looking *good* doesn't always mean looking *right*. To engineer an effective match, to make yourself truly attractive to the person you like, and to keep the relationship fresh and successful in the weeks, months or years that follow, you will need to be skilled at both reading and transmitting the hidden signals of sexual bodytalk.

How This Book Works

By explaining this process of what does and doesn't attract, and by analysing certain key aspects that you probably thought were random, this book will help you understand this vital process of unspoken sexual communication. Then, by learning vital tips and techniques, you will find out how to make your own sensual and emotional charisma more effective.

To have true sex appeal to a potential partner you will need to begin a ritual of successful silent communication that creates echoes reaching back to their childhood and even beyond. Some techniques are instinctive, others more sophisticated, but all can be enhanced with understanding and practice. Sending, reading and understanding these signals will enable you to improve your ability to make the right 'connections' with the conscious and subconscious mind of someone you like.

This book will give you help throughout each stage of the meeting/dating/mating ritual, showing you how to make the most of yourself through:

- A bodytalk make-over. You'll learn quick-fix tips to make you look more attractive instantly, from fixing your posture and the way you walk to how to smile, use eye contact and move your hands, torso and legs.

- Creating empathy – understanding the subtle signals to get on his/her wavelength instantly.

- Appealing on every level.

- Avoiding the turn-offs. You'll discover what body language gestures turn most men and women off instantly, and how to eliminate them from your repertoire.

- Flirting – without looking like Dick Emery in drag.

- Listening – your own body language signals are only 50 per cent of the communication process; reading your partner's messages will help you understand him/her better.

- Touching.

- Learning to read your long-term partner and avoiding the pitfalls of stereotype and assumption.

- Using eye *and* ear listening.

- Learning how to tell whether he/she's having an affair.

- Learning how to *have* an affair.

- Adding zest to your relationship – without the aid of bondage parties.

Sex Signals will also provide an insight into key areas such as:

- Who am I attracted to, and why?

- What sexual signals is my body sending out to other people?

- How can I make myself more effective at sending out positive signals of attraction?

- How can I tell if he/she fancies me?

- How can I manage that first meeting, and what are the vital aspects of positive initial contact?

- How can I strike a balance between playing it too cool and coming on too strong?

- What sex-signal changes occur in a long-term relationship, and how can I adjust to make sure the attraction between us is kept alive?

- How can I tell when things start to go seriously wrong in a relationship?

- What are the rituals of sex signals during sex itself? How can I tell what my partner wants, or work towards enhanced mutual pleasure without using awkward verbal requests?

Two-way Transmissions

Sex Signals will show you how to both read and transmit successful non-verbal communication. This can be tricky at the best of times, but during sexual encounters it can become mangled to the point of being farcical. Embarrassment and fear of failure scupper even the most basic skills.

First meetings can be especially woeful. Like a candidate at a job interview, we want to impress instantly and constantly, and this leads to pressure and even stress, which in turn can lead to our displaying a chronic lack of sophistication and know-how. We mishear, misinterpret and misunderstand. Nervousness and a lack of confidence constitute one of life's biggest banana skins. The harder we worry about what others are thinking, the more we slip, totter and – ultimately – fall on our bum.

The list of inhibiting factors is endless, and yet a vast portion of our lives is dedicated to finding the perfect partner. No wonder we need help. And that is exactly what this book offers.

Updating the Dating Process

In recent years we have undergone a quiet revolution in terms of meeting and dating, and as these cultural changes occur it is important to update your skills to keep in line. For instance, 40 per cent of us now claim to have met a partner in the workplace. Office romances are now less likely to be frowned on by bosses. These days we have many new ways to flirt and pair off, including the Internet, e-mail, text messages and speed-dating agencies. Women have become less passive and more proactive about finding a man. Getting married has increased in popularity, but so has getting divorced. People are less likely to 'retire' from the dating market in middle or old age.

Passing through the Age Barrier

This is not just a book for first-time daters. During the course of a lifetime both men and women go through several sexual stages, from the nervous, spotty-teenager phase through to mature, long-lasting relationships. In modern society getting old is no longer an option, and neither – often – is the idea of partnerships for life.

Rising divorce rates mean that, far from settling into some stage of stable sexual maturity, people in middle age and beyond are now finding themselves plunged into the partner-seeking marketplace many times over, often with as little or less confidence than they had when they were 15.

This book will help you through all these critical – and often amusing – stages by providing an insight into all the unspoken communication skills needed to navigate them successfully. By reading the human body language signals of others, while monitoring your own, you can begin to control your attempts to meet, flirt, date, seduce and mate with total success.

CHAPTER ONE

Bodytalk: The Four Key Barriers

So why do we need training in body language? Surely it is one of the core animal survival skills that we were born with and have grown up honing and perfecting?

In a way this is true, although as we struggle through early life and start trying to *plan* how to behave, rather than acting spontaneously, we are taught two aspects of conditioned behaviour that act like industrial-strength weed-killer on those small budding shoots of non-verbal talent: we learn how to talk and we learn how to lie. From then on – in terms of mastering body language signals – it can be downhill all the way.

Although not a precise science, body language has become a largely untapped and neglected skill in terms of effective communication and understanding. You were great at it as a kid. Your pets excel at it. And yet humans 'develop' to a point where they find verbal communication more intellectually rewarding.

When we transmit and receive sex signals, though, we rarely place much emphasis on the words someone uses, mainly because our other senses, especially the visual and olfactory ones, take over. In so far as we do pay attention to the spoken word, vocal tone is far more appealing than verbal content, unless the person you are listening to is using words like 'I won the lottery last week'. In normal, non-sexual communication, tone of voice accounts for 38 per cent of the impact, which is why a voice can be seductive if the tone and pitch are seen as appealing.

So, given that bodytalk is such a dominant form of communication, why is it that most humans are painfully unaware of their own signals, and equally confused by those of others around them? What exactly *are* all the barriers that help scupper this most basic of skills?

To find out you need to go right back to your first attempts at communication, namely:

Babytalk

Life was pretty simple when you were a baby. Born into a state of fearlessness and spontaneity, you were by far the least equipped of any animal to support and nurture yourself. So while you lay there in your cot, waiting helplessly for the next plate of mashed pear, you – in conjunction with nature – developed a cunning survival plan. You would make the big people *want* to fetch and carry for you by looking cute. Your big, round eyes, chubby cheeks and little bald head would make you instantly disarming (beware – this appeal pales in later life). To guarantee the adults' attention in the first place you would cry to an extent that was virtually impossible to ignore. Later you would develop this into the mini-drama known as throwing a tantrum in public.

From the age of about 15 minutes you were reading body language signals to see whether your ploys were working. At that age you even began mimicking your mother's facial expressions to gain acceptance, while the cast of your features led relatives to say 'Doesn't he/she look like his/her daddy?' to ensure bonding with and protection and nurture from the one not always guaranteed to be 100 per cent certain of blood parentage.

So, from the moment of birth your survival techniques consisted of appealing to your parents by getting their attention through being loud, then looking cute, then copying their body movements to create empathy.

Simple? Of course.

Effective? Absolutely.

And if this very basic survival technique sounds familiar, it could be that you kept to this winning formula of 'Attract attention to gain approval' in later life. Only this time your goal was more than mere personal survival; you were also hell-bent on the survival of your entire species – in other words, you were primarily after sex.

Unfortunately, by then factors had kicked in to make this simplistic and successful formula more complex and unreliable. You were an outstanding graduate of the school of bodytalk until around the age of three, which is almost exactly when four key barriers began to appear. These are:

1 Being told 'It's rude to stare'

Your own current ability to read the vital non-verbal signals of people around you has been scuppered by this one phrase, which haunted your early years. This simple sentence – probably uttered by your embarrassed parents on a regular basis until you got the message – created one of the biggest barriers holding back your present-day communication skills. Monitoring non-verbal signals effectively, as nature intended you to, requires watching. Which is – unfortunately – socially unacceptable. Excessive use of eye contact leads inevitably to aggression. 'Who're you looking at?' is the battle cry of the pub punch-up. Staring is unsettling, even to non-strangers. Try staring at your partner for longer than usual and watch how quickly he/she becomes paranoid and starts asking what's wrong.

There is a strange perversity about the fact that the only person we stare at for long periods of time is the person we are in love with. Study a couple at a restaurant table and you will soon see what stage their relationship is at. Extended eye-gazing displays tend to signal the stage that extends from first falling in love up to co-habitation. The perversity lies in the fact that it would be more useful if we could stare at potential partners long before we start to fall in love with them. The staring would help us monitor who they are and what they are like. But staring is an intimacy only lovers can share, constantly checking each facial movement for signs of approval or disapproval to render themselves as pleasing as possible all the time.

So you have had to develop a system of reading without

looking. You glance, you peek, and you use peripheral vision. Which means you miss a lot.

Then there is the second barrier, known as:

2 Masking (or lying)

Masking is a form of polite trickery that prevents us revealing ourselves to others. To be good at reading sexual body language you'll have to learn to read between the lines a lot. Humans – unlike most animals – feel a sense of social responsibility as regards their body language signals. We avoid the overtly honest or coarse and opt for trickery, denial and lie. While two dogs will happily sniff bottoms to make a sexual assessment, humans feel that this technique is way down the scale in terms of the successful chat-up. We will, however, cheerfully signal a complete lack of interest when we first meet someone we fancy, putting this odd technique under the label of 'playing it cool'.

Another reason for masking our true feelings is fear of rejection. Most of us want to leave the exit door well ajar before committing ourselves even to the idea that we are attracted to the other person, and this can lead to a whole raft of confusing and dishonest body language signals. We hint and play peek-a-boo. We delay the final moment when our stall is set out in open view and we dare to commit, even to an 'I quite fancy you, actually'. We joke, we flirt and we pave the way for sex, and all the time we have that excuse or one-liner ready in case of a knock-back. We look for congruence and empathy when we read the other person's body language signals, but without ever offering a clear display of our own feelings. Even when we commit to sex we often require the full range of options for relationship refusal before, during and after the act itself.

When we converse with someone, though, we are greatly affected by that person's sincerity, or lack of it. We like to get behind the social signals and take a peek at the *real* meaning of their words. This is all part of getting to know someone better. In sexual encounters that knowledge is usually seen as vital, especially if a long-term relationship is on the cards. Which is why congruence is important. When your words, tone and non-verbal signals all say the same thing you will appear honest to other people, and therefore more likeable. So social 'masking' – hiding our true feelings through a sense of etiquette and a fear of rejection – causes problems in the very earliest stages of a sexual relationship. And yet it remains a necessity if we don't want to appear stupid, gauche or rude – or even threatening. Our early conditioning tells us that we should avoid the more spontaneous sexual signals and start playing body language games, like feigning indifference or playing it cool.

The third barrier can be described as:

3 Sexual discrepancies (the Mars/Venus conundrum)

There is often a complete mismatch in both verbal and visual messaging between the two sexes, due to upbringing and many unfathomable differences in our communication styles. (You can begin to see why we need help to unravel the fascinating and complex strands of sexual signalling.)

Men are – in general – baffled by the signals sent out by women, and the same applies the other way round. On a good day this can lead to comical misunderstandings, while on a bad day it can mean relationship breakdown and genuine tragedy.

Embarrassment and an inability to translate male/female signals render verbal messaging virtually useless, not only in the early stages of meeting, when we might attract by looks and movement alone, but also through the later stages, during the sex act itself.

Sadly (and sometimes amusingly), when it comes to the male/female non-verbal sexual communication process, experience doesn't always mean enhanced expertise. Long-term marrieds are often just as baffled by their partner's sexual behaviour as those on a first date. Unfortunately the desire to make sense of all the confusion will often lead to stereotyping or ignoring vital signals and responses – often to the detriment of the relationship itself.

Finally, there is the fourth barrier:

4 The etiquette of sex

The last key barrier to open and accessible body language during the meeting/mating process is adherence to the social sexual rules. These are the guidelines according to which we agree to play the game. By and large our parents or peers teach them to us, and they dictate what is 'right' behaviour and what is socially 'wrong'.

Like all other forms of etiquette, they put a bit of a damper on our natural, animal responses. For instance, a girl might fancy the pants off a boy, but cultural requirements may mean that she will feign a lack of interest in having sex with him until the third or fourth date, or even until marriage.

Most youngsters grow up with an idea of how quickly or slowly you should make each sexual move, from first kissing to body touching to full sex. These 'rules' may entail a struggle with natural instinct, and an even greater struggle with communication signals. Break the rules, though, and you will appear at best clumsy and at worst a sex pest or a pervert. In the business environment these rules may be officially sanctioned under the heading 'sexual harassment'.

Often we have trouble recognising whether someone fancies us or not. Are they failing to register attraction through a lack of interest, or through a sense of etiquette? So the question has to be asked: how do you distinguish between someone who is 'playing it cool', fearing rejection, or merely following etiquette, and someone who finds you about as appealing as an overdue VAT return?

Overcoming the Barriers: Reading between the Lines

The key to overcoming those four key bodytalk barriers is simple. As you progress through the book you are going to learn how to become more receptive and perceptive. You can't sit and stare. But you can start to look for certain ritualistic signals. Even a quick glance can provide you with a great deal of information, as long as you know what you are looking for.

When you listen to people, use your eyes as well as your ears. Listening is a skill that is *active*, not passive. Your skills of perception are probably suffering from severe neglect. The frequency of our transactions with others makes us speed up the process of alerting ourselves to their sexual and non-sexual signals to the point where they become senseless. Become more careful and more analytical. Be alert to the message behind the words. Stop obsessing about your own messages and open yourself to others' unspoken dialogues.

When you see someone, try to work out what mood they are in. How are they feeling? How do these feelings change throughout your transaction? Forget the words, as they are low-impact. We are all trained from childhood to say the right thing. Our mouths deal in clichés; our bodies reveal what is fresh and honest.

Try to look behind the mask – consider words and facial expressions just as part of the 'presenting' personality. What we see is often the social front. When you study the smaller gestures and expressions you will often discover the feelings behind the mask. Work down through the layers. Remember, you may not be talking the same language, so keep an open mind. The ability to translate is vital.

To make the process easier for you, we are going to analyse the meet/date/mate process step by step, supplying tips and techniques to help at every stage.

CHAPTER TWO

The Secrets of Instant Attraction

Before you begin learning to read and transmit more effective love/lust/maybe-just-start-with-a-quick-drink-and-then-I'll-think-about-it signals, it's important to understand exactly what it is that might make you attractive to another person in the first place.

And if the thoughts 'Big tits' or 'A fat wallet' just floated through your mind, then you won't be surprised to know that you *could* be right, although not in most cases. Life is never that simple, not even when it comes to sex.

So what is it about you that can draw one person but turn another off? What are the factors that will lead to sexual or emotional attraction, or even love at first sight? Understanding which of these factors will make someone else fancy you underpins all the work involved in enhancing your techniques to achieve success.

The secrets of what makes you attractive *to* and attracted *by* others can appear random and unfathomable. And yet there is a way of cracking the code. Much of what turns us on or off is based on repeat patterns of comfort, love and sexuality that have been programmed into us since our childhood. And many of these patterns are signalled through our body language.

To understand the qualities in *you* that will hopefully attract a potential mate, you can do no better than study the things that make you fancy someone else. Did you ever meet someone you fell for instantly? Have you ever stood in a crowded room and felt an almost physical pull towards a complete stranger? Did you wonder why your mind and body had singled out that particular individual? Was it love or lust – or both?

Perhaps they were 'socially suitable' – someone who would be judged to be good looking by most people. But then you see good-looking people every day, so why this one? Or maybe they were plain or downright ugly, because physical attraction isn't always governed by the social 'ideal'. Even close friends who grow up with what appears to be a shared taste in men or women can often find themselves falling eventually for someone the rest of the group find achingly unattractive.

You may already have experienced this divergence in the shared sexual tastes of the 'pack' yourself. Have you ever had to mask your surprise/horror/naked repulsion when a pal you thought you knew well turned up at your house clinging adoringly to a bit of a minger with a personality to match? Have you ever been asked 'So what do you think of him?' and had to bite back comments like 'Well, if he'd trim his nasal hair a bit I might be able to get a better look'? The point is your friend *did* find him attractive, even if you didn't. Which means she was looking at something *you* didn't see, because your life experiences are different to hers. The hairy nostrils you found so repulsive could even have been her greatest turn-on. Yes, really! Perhaps they reminded her of nostrils she had known and loved in her past.

In essence, superficial attraction is governed by social ideals of looks and behaviour, but to be deeply attractive to a potential partner you will have to work your way through much deeper layers of animal instinct and emotional baggage. While social attraction values can easily be shared – hence the appeal of, say, Brad Pitt or Halle Berry to a very wide international and multi-cultural audience – genuine, long-lasting attraction is individual, and based on complex values. You have your own blueprint, and so does the person you fancy.

Levels of Attraction

Keeping this blueprint in mind, to attract someone in a way that will make them feel as though a two-ton truck has just made contact with their lower intestine – to engender love at first sight – you will have to appeal to them on four vital levels:

1 The social/conditioned level

The appeal of stereotypical good looks – the Barbie/Ken factor
– is primarily a matter of social success. The question they will
ask as they look at you is: 'Will this person be acceptable to my
friends/family/pack?', or even: 'Will the pack be impressed or
jealous when they see what I have pulled? Will this person
make *me* seem more acceptable?') These are questions
prompted by ego, by a desire to sustain, increase or enhance
social status by proxy.

Women tend to be less swayed by visual impressions than
men, which often makes us easier to please in the looks
department. Why? Well, because we are optimistic make-over
specialists. In essence we are the Carole Smillies of the mating
process. If the social fit is poor, if a man is aesthetically chal-
lenged, a women will often assess his potential for change and
improvement – a little like a house-buyer looking over an older
property with renovation in mind. Can he be groomed and
tidied up? Will his flat look more savoury after redecoration?
Might he be trained out of eating with his mouth open?

Men, on the other hand, tend to be visual pessimists, which
makes this quality of instant social attraction more important
to them. Most of them have less flair for redesign and renovation. If a woman looks good, a man will assume that this is as
good as it gets. If anything, he suspects she will 'go off' once he
marries her. Men tend to have a habit of looking at a girl's
mother to see what lies in store. They become gloomy and
imagine we will stop bleaching our roots and start bulging at
the thighs the minute they are on the hook.

Yes, men *do* work out in gyms and keep themselves trim and
youthful looking. But somewhere in the back of their minds is
the idea that not doing so is not necessarily risking scuppering
their chances of being seen as sexy and attractive. Baldness,
beer bellies and wrinkles still somehow seem to count as 'desirable', even on a global stage – consider Hollywood, where the
likes of Sean Connery, Jack Nicholson, Robert De Niro and
even Woody Allen may still be cast as potential lust buckets.

If you study the current examples of the male sexual 'ideal'
paraded in film, press and advertising, you could be forgiven
for coming to the conclusion that men find the lure of the

female 'ideal' stereotype much more irresistible than the 'perfect' male might be to women. Throughout history, the concept of the male 'ideal' fantasy has held true. There have seemingly always been women who are attractive to most men, purely because of their good looks, rather than by virtue of intellect or personality.

These 'desirable' women form a potent stereotype. Other women will often try to emulate their style of good looks, even going so far as to disfigure their bodies in an attempt to do so. Often the original stereotype herself will have achieved her 'universally desirable' features only through similar bouts of plastic surgery. So Pamela Anderson has plastic surgery to become Pamela Anderson, who then gets copied by thousands of women wanting to copy the Pamela Anderson blend of fat-free body and vastly over-generous breasts. Even porn stars have a similar size and shape stereotype. With very few 'specialist' exceptions, these women are unfeasibly tiny, apart from their breasts. The rule is that they should have no other body fat. For the male stars, though, stamina seems more important than shape.

Beauty contests for women, like Miss World, are feasible only because of this global stereotyping, which deems women's ability to be attractive to men to be mathematically measurable, the vital statistics being quantified in terms of age, height, bust, waist and hips. To describe a women in terms that other men will find attractive, a guy need only recite that she is aged 16 to 25, with a figure measuring 36-24-34, or thereabouts. (Some will even quote cup size to add subtlety to the image – 36DD would probably sound about right to get other eyes bulging.) Women who get to the top as Hollywood icons are often both extremely beautiful *and* in possession of wonderful bodies, like Halle Berry, Nicole Kidman and Jennifer Lopez.

Women, however, seem to be less focused when it comes to the link between stereotypical good looks and attraction in a man. Male icons will vary tremendously in terms of age and appearance. If we are presented with an example of 'beauty-by-numbers' we are more likely to laugh at it than want to idolise it. Real beauties, like Johnny Depp or Jude Law – and Terence Stamp before them – have almost certainly had to take roles that cast them against type – for example, as dangerous psychopaths or weirdos – to avoid this trap of being seen purely as cheesecake, and therefore turning women off.

Men who pursue the beefcake image, like Schwarzenegger, Stallone and Segal, have been cast in 'male' adventure films rather than women's erotica. This lack of a 'measurable male' icon most likely accounts for the lack of female-oriented porn. Open any men's mag on the top shelf and you'll see that exhausting array of super-slim bodies and large breasts. If you tried to invent a similarly successful formula for women's mags you'd quickly be left floundering.

So, bearing the 'social ideal' scenario in mind, why is it that women are traditionally still supposed to be turned on by old slobs?

But are we in fact sure that men aren't the same? When did they get offered a female sex icon that didn't fit the stereotypical mould? Perhaps it's the fault of the people who make films and ads. Perhaps men are in fact crying out for a large, grey-haired older woman with wrinkles to seduce that nice young Brad Pitt in a movie. Perhaps the same moguls who cast Connery alongside Zeta-Jones in a recent film would also like to make one where Judi Dench bags Leonardo Di Caprio and it's all seen as kosher.

This female open-mindedness about men's looks does seem to be changing, though. Men's magazines that focus on grooming and health tips are on the increase. Women are beginning to expect levels of physical perfection similar to those they themselves are supposed to achieve. Clear, youthful skin and a firm six-pack are rapidly becoming the norm, rather than the exception.

Gay men are traditionally known for investing more time and effort in looking good than straight men. And what emerges? A fit-looking, well-shaped stereotype whose aim (like that of straight women) is to appeal to other men.

And while we're on the subject of looks, don't forget that you might need to qualify in a rather different way visually if you've set your cap at a perennial cutie on the dating circuit: the Narcissistic Partner.

In most people like attracts like, but the narcissist has an even stricter agenda – he/she sees a mirror image and it will appear instantly adorable. I don't need to tell you that this stems from an over-abundance of self-love. (Still, it makes a change from paranoia and low self-esteem.) Look at many famous couples and what do you see? Peas in a pod. They take on the same mannerisms as one another, they wear the same type of clothes, they have similar haircuts, and they start looking as though they're worked by the same set of strings. Famous morphees have included:

- Posh and Becks (same clothes and taste in jewellery)

- Brad Pitt and Gwyneth Paltrow (identical haircuts)

- Michael Douglas and Catherine Zeta-Jones (same regal air)

- Liz Hurley and Hugh Grant (similar features and attitude)

Why the attraction in looking alike? Well, there could be a couple of reasons.

Like-bodied tends to translate as like-minded. It's the comfort of the familiar again. Looking alike and acting alike can fast-track empathy. You feel you know the other person already. You think you might share the same taste in everything, including sex.

Alternatively, as we have mentioned, like can be attracted to like if 'like' likes him/herself a little too much. You may appeal as a body double of that person. When they gaze into your eyes or admire your body, it might be the closest they get to looking in the mirror ...

There is another intriguing facet of mutual attraction and the 'social' ideal. It is an obvious rule of life that some people are better looking than others – which could imply that the beautiful will inherit the earth and that ugly-bugs will be left without a mate in life.

Not true.

When we look around for a mate we will often seek out someone at our own level of attractiveness. Now you might think that this means that we are settling for second best, but that's not always the case. Nature will often urge us to seek out these visual soulmates and to actually prefer them to their more beautiful friends. A real-life line-up of male or female supermodels might impress our sense of orderly beauty, just as a work of art would, but we might not find them actively attractive. They might just not press the right buttons.

Sour grapes? Maybe. Your average supermodel might be sending out the wrong body language signals for the obvious reasons (because they find mere mortals about as attractive as second-hand toilet paper and therefore don't bother to send out any flirt signals whatsoever), which may render them 'non-attractive' in the flesh. Your logical mind may also be labelling them as 'non-attractive' as a warning, the message being: 'Could you cope with the fact that everyone else will be attracted to this person as well? How long could you stand the competition?'

If your childhood patterns require you to be the centre of attention, you may also register this person as 'non-attractive' because you couldn't stand having to take a back seat. Maybe you are used to being the most beautiful person around. And maybe that's the way you feel most comfortable and how you would like the situation to stay. By dating someone with superior looks you could feel that your own visual supremacy is compromised. So you seek out someone you see as being at your own level of physical good looks. It may be this which first sparks your interest – it is often the first step in singling someone out.

To attract a 'social' match, then, you will need to present yourself in a way that will have strong visual appeal to both your partner and his/her social pack. This will mean you being a close visual equal – as good looking as your target – or even that you might need to look very similar. And if you are a man, you are more likely to trade up in beauty terms than if you are a woman.

2 Evolutional/genetic level
Another crucial value in most people's criteria of what attracts and what doesn't is: Will this person provide me with healthy offspring?

The desire to mate is a strong one, obviously. We have sex to bond, and to have fun, and to procreate. (Or maybe even to earn a living, if that is your choice of career.) Your potential partner will be rating your value in terms of all three, even if the last option is unlikely or unpopular on a conscious level. You will be studied for signs of good health and breeding potential (except in single-sex relationships).

They will also want to know whether you will be sexually attractive in a very individual way. Will you turn them on? Will you mate in their own preferred style? Will you turn them on sexually in ways that go far beyond the realms of social attraction?

This is where the social factors tend to wane. When we get down to the serious business of mating and procreating, most of us are aware that we will at some stage move away from our pack and isolate ourselves as a couple. Therefore the pack's approval of our choice will – for most – come to nought eventually if we aren't genuinely turned on sexually as an individual by our choice of mate. And long term this problem can only get worse.

Your first sexual interest or arousal will have created strong trace patterns in your subconscious. Who or what were you first attracted to? (I say 'what' because I believe I had a bit of a crush on one of the puppets from *Thunderbirds* for a short while in my murky childhood, which may well account for at least a couple of dodgy partnership choices later on in life.) These early stirrings can guide your tastes throughout your life.

Then there is the issue of sensory awareness and sensory appeal. It is important to appeal to your prospective partner's dominant sense. Smell, touch, hearing, taste and sight can all be stimulated by a mate, but most of us will have one sense that is dominant. This dominant sense forms a very potent trigger in your ability to be attractive and attracted to someone else.

Here is a way to discover your own. Close your eyes and relax. Blank your mind out for a few moments and then try to think back to a time in your childhood when you were really happy. Spend a while reliving this experience in your memory. Then open your eyes and describe it to yourself. Remember which of your senses was most responsible for the pleasure. Did you *see* yellow sand and the sun glinting off the ocean? Did you *hear* seagulls or children's laughter? Did you *feel* the sun on your face or the warm sand between your toes? Did you *smell* the perfume of flowers? Could you *taste* the candyfloss or ice cream?

Whichever sense came to the forefront was probably your most dominant. This sense will need to be stimulated for you to find someone truly attractive, and equally for someone to be attracted to you.

The attractors might include:

- *Aural:* your vocal tone

- *Visual:* your colouring and the clothes you choose to wear

- *Tactile:* how your skin and body feel to the touch; the firmness of your flesh and the shape of your body

- *Olfactory:* how your body and hair smell and the perfume or cologne you use

So, to attract an evolutional match you may have to display levels of good health (clear, glowing skin, good teeth, glossy hair, etc.), fitness and sexuality. Your sensual signals – the way you move, touch and flirt – will all create a sexual aura that can attract or repel a future partner.

3 Emotional level

We all seek emotional 'strokes' from a new relationship. These are the rewards and comforts that come from conversation and behaviour. In a sexual relationship the key question will be: Will you make this person happy (or even *unhappy*, depending on the familiar patterns from his/her childhood)?

How can they start to find out? Well, often by honing in on repeat patterns of love, comfort and emotion that were created in childhood. These patterns are often locked away in the deepest levels of the subconscious, sometimes so deep that we are unaware of their very existence. The conscious brain is often baffled when they surface and start to dominate decisions and choices. They are traces of memories and behaviours, forming what is often a blatant attempt to re-create the ghosts of the past and turn them into the future.

These shady echoes often reflect flawed assumptions about past success, though. In a bid to re-create comfort, or repeat patterns of love, people often seek out the familiar, even when that pattern of relationship was heavily dysfunctional, which is often why you will see someone with a history of repeat relationships with alcoholics, or wife-beaters. Each time they leave a dangerous and flawed relationship they swear never to make the same mistake again, and yet often they do.

Patterns from the past are hard to suppress, because they are illogically associated with comfort and love. People spot traces that they recognise, and blindly follow them down familiar paths, often without question. Familiarity may breed contempt, but it can also breed dumb tolerance, as well.

To illustrate: have you ever get lost several times on a journey? The consequences of this can often be very similar to those that occur when people seek out dysfunctional life patterns. If you made the same mistakes again after getting lost the first time the chances are you took the same wrong turnings because all your brain was telling you was that the roads looked familiar – you didn't know whether any particular road was wrong or right, only that you'd taken it before.

This 'familiarity with the past' is the same sense that can drive us to choose a particular partner, or find them attractive. It is as though a blueprint of the 'perfect' man or woman has been etched into our brains before we have the logical capacity to question it. It can become established as 'normal'. There are qualities there that will always have a strong draw for you, even when your conscious mind tells you that the surface attraction is minimal or even non-existent.

Never underestimate the power of subconscious thought. When the conscious and subconscious are in conflict, it is the subconscious which invariably wins, which is why certain physical traits will be attractive to your subconscious but not to your conscious mind. You might, for instance, link large hips or chubby knees in a woman or a beer belly or a big nose in a man with a feeling of comfort, security and love if the features are familiar from your past.

This is your sexual trip-switch, then, taking its cues from

childhood and beyond. There are visual triggers and events that we associate with sexual arousal and/or patterns of love or security. You may be attracted to someone who looks like a parent, or even someone who looks very much like *you*, in which case these factors will bring out a feeling of security in you. If, however, you are turned on by feelings of *insecurity*, if you prefer fear and danger in a sexual relationship, you may well find yourself attracted by someone who looks and behaves in a way that is completely alien to you.

Does this mean you will have to look like his/her mother/father to be attractive? In reality, probably not – although, thinking about it, in some cases you could do worse. It may well be that your potential partner is secretly on the prowl for someone who presents the complete antithesis of their parent's values – a 'mummy-shocker', guaranteed to get a negative response from the old folks at home, whether through their partner's navel piercing, their transsexual outfits or the fact that they have a mouth like a fishwife's. The key moment for the mummy-shocker is taking the new partner back to the suburban bungalow for tea. You don't need a degree in psycho-analysis to realise that this is the act of the rebellious child buried deep – or maybe not so deep – now seeking to punish the parent. This may not be the best fight-to-the-death to get yourself involved in, especially if you are looking for some-thing long-term and secure. Your intended partner may use you as little more than the nearest implement they can find to batter their parents with. By choosing you, this person may feel an initial sense of euphoria and release from the binds of their childhood. So if you want to be used as living therapy, go ahead.

To appeal on this emotional level, then, you will need to display the potential to repeat patterns from the other person's childhood. These links are complex and difficult to simulate. However, watching the other person over time should reveal clues to deep-rooted emotional needs. Respond in an appropri-ate way (as long as you are happy with any necessary tailoring of your own behaviour) and you could form a match as a couple.

4 Logical/intellectual level

This is the dry, crusty old voice of reason and objectivity which strives to create order and calm when you go into emotional overdrive. It looks for intellectual and financial bonding. If you are a woman, it may well be on the hunt for someone who can give you financial security. It will warn you of factors like marital status and physical proximity: 'He's married and lives on the other side of the world', say. It evaluates potential success based on statistics and logic. (Although it tends to become less assertive with each alcoholic drink you down.)

If you like what you see at first glance, you will often start to make enquiries about the more practical aspects of any union. Are they married or single? What's their background? What's their relationship history? Where do they live? What sort of job do they have? What type of car? If they live with their parents, drive a three-wheeler and have no dates notched up so far, you might still make the stretch if the social and/or evolutional/instinctive responses are dominant and recording a high score.

Women can be attracted to wealth and power. This could be seen as an appeal to logic. Perhaps the woman feels that the powerful and/or rich man will be able to care for her and her child better than the handsome impoverished man. If a man is good looking *and* powerful and/or wealthy, perhaps her logical brain tells her that the combination may be too seductive to other women. If he is powerful but not handsome, perhaps she will be able to keep her protector for as long as she likes.

But isn't the idea of the woman being in need of protection from a strong male a little hackneyed by now? Surely the concept of power as an aphrodisiac should either have become non-sexist by now, with acceptance of the idea of the powerful woman being equally attractive to men, or it should have faded in favour of good looks. But has that really happened?

Certainly the implication that women are particularly in need of protection in modern society *is* an outdated idea. The only scenario in which 'power' is still a factor is in the workplace, where the boss–employee male–female relationship is still alive and kicking, and still founded on the attraction of power rather than looks.

Does female power attract male subordinates in the same way in the workplace scenario? Unfortunately the jury is still out on that one. Women are making inroads into management roles, but still mainly in departments where they have been traditionally prevalent, like Human Resources. But if powerful female bosses did turn on subordinate men, would these same women be attracted 'downward'? Or would they prefer a mate of equal or higher status?

Madonna is one example of the powerful woman whom men find attractive. Many of her earlier relationships were of the 'downward' type. Her marriage to Sean Penn was nearly a meeting of equals, although it was obvious that their wedding would never have elicited such a media flurry if it had been Sean Penn marrying someone else. Madonna's status was far superior in that marriage. Her marriage to Guy Ritchie is interesting. Again, Madonna is by far the more senior in status, although Guy could appear superior to her in the sphere she apparently wants to work more in, which is movies. The other facet of this union is that they are both good-looking people, so any power imbalance would be offset by the sense of social attraction.

But we also need to consider the idea of 'social power'. Some people have a tendency to dominate whatever social group they find themselves in. If the domination is natural, and the person isn't taking the lead through bullying, boring or displaying arrogance, this social skill can be labelled 'charisma'. Charisma is a very attractive quality in both men and women.

Watch any group of people and you will find one who naturally emerges as leader. This leadership may not be constant; there may be an ebb and flow, depending on new characters joining the group. When the gathering is business based, the 'leader' will normally be chosen by rank and status, rather than social skills. But even in this type of group a more natural leader can emerge. People listen when they speak, and agree with them; there is a natural respect from the rest of the group. When an opinion or decision is wanted, the others will generally turn to this person to hear what they have to say. They don't have to fight for attention, like less charismatic characters.

Watch the body language set pieces to see who is the natural leader in a group. When they speak the others will turn their heads to listen, signalling full attention. They will tend to instigate changes of posture, too. Watch to see who in a group moves first and how the rest fall in line. This natural social dominance can be very attractive. (Which is why there are tips on honing the skill later in this book.)

Another feature of this 'leadership' charisma is that it feels very nice to be the one in this position, which is why many women use body language skills to promote this feeling in their man. Watch some female partners in a social situation – when the man speaks they give him their undivided attention and provide a good audience, even if it is an audience of one. This 'Nancy Reagan' approach is blatant man-flattery but it works, not only because the attention massages the ego, but also as a signal in the social structure. The gestures advertise the fact that this man would be a good group leader. It is a great enhancer, but one rarely used by men on women.

Conversely, in a relationship that has less going for it, there will be an aspect of social lowering in one partner's approach to the other. When one partner speaks the other is ready to butt in, look distracted or feel obliged to 'put the record straight'. This kind of behaviour is a non-attractor, guaranteed either to start an argument or – if it is still being used as a factor in sexual attraction – to lower the partner's self-esteem to the point where he/she will feel grateful to the other person for even staying with them.

So, to attract on the logical level you will have to display a degree of power, status and/or wealth that is compatible with the other person's needs.

Matching Objectives

So what other factors will make you attractive to a potential mate? Love at first sight is all very well if it's love which you or your potential partner are looking for, but what if what you're after is something shallower and more fun? Another aspect of your compatibility on first meeting will be your ability to create an intentional match of relationship objectives.

What is your objective in attracting someone? Are you looking for a partner for life, or a night of one-off, mind-boggling sex? Do you want someone to take home to meet your mother, or someone all your mates will be lusting after?

Body language clues are often sent out on first meeting to discover whether your intentions match or not. Time is a precious commodity, and modern life decrees that we waste as little as possible, which is why these 'intentional' signals are becoming more blatant. Some people might use them as a means to an end – say, pretending to be looking for love when all they want is a quick fun screw and no fuss afterwards in case their husband/wife finds out. But generally these intentional gestures are more overt now that virginity and marriage are less of an issue. Being perceptive about them leads to time-efficient pairing-off.

We tend to temper our signals to suit the type of relationship we are looking for, and a mismatch can be fatal. Often it is just a case of being the right person in the right place at the wrong time. You might meet your ideal long-term love match at a moment when your signals indicate you are looking for fun sex on a plate. You might over-play the flirt signals to the point where the potential love of your life is put off because he/she gets the message that you are too readily available, and there-fore not the kind of 'settling down' partner he/she is currently looking for. Sometimes it's a good idea to leave mating 'busi-ness' cards, enabling you to get back in touch with each other when your relationship objectives are more compatible.

So, this is the essence of the secret of attraction.

And love at first sight? How is that particular phenomenon created?

Easy – this 'perfect' matching will occur when all the levels appear compatible. This will make you look like someone's dream date. If – visually and instantly – you appear 'right' in terms of all the other person's attraction levels, then you will find yourself scoring a one-way hit. If their appearance does the same for you then your behaviour will confirm this instant attraction and – hey presto! – love at first sight.

CHAPTER THREE

The First Impression: How to Create Instant Attraction

Keeping in mind the factors involved in attraction, how can you walk into a bar, club or party and be appealing to anyone you like? Well, sadly, the answer has to be that you probably can't. Very few people manage to pull off being drop-dead gorgeous to *all* around them. As we saw in the last chapter, to create a genuine 'match' with someone you will need to be very specific with your target, as long-lasting attachments often require a unique blend of attraction factors.

However, you *can* enhance your ability to target a wider range of people and make yourself more 'globally gorgeous'. The secret is all in the way you present yourself to the room in general and what 'first-glance' signals you then send out.

Like a baby using its instinctive survival techniques, to succeed you must first attract someone's attention and then look appealing to them, for which you need to understand the science of the First Impression, which takes as little as three seconds to create – the time required to sum another person up in our high-speed modern society. Most of it is based on what we are seeing. Vocal tone may get a look-in, but we mainly judge from things like facial expression and body movement.

When we first glance at another person our evolutionary programming requires us to check whether they constitute a potential threat to us. Following this 'fight or flight' enquiry, we may well start to decide whether we would like to mate with them or not. In an alarmingly short space of time we reach a conclusion as to whether someone is of any sexual interest to us, or not. If the answer is that they are not, then they come under the category we will call the Deletions.

First you will need to attract the eye of this other person, and then you will need to stay off their deletions list. Even then you will be a long way away from the decision to bond.

Getting Noticed

High social attractors do well at this point because their visual appeal will stop most pairs of eyes in their tracks.

Charisma is another way to draw attention positively. Charismatic people tend to radiate confidence and an interest in their surroundings.

Sexuality will be another draw. Even relatively unattractive people can use sexually explicit clothes or sensual body movements to command attention.

Power, fame or status can be another draw. People who are 'known', or who dominate a group by virtue of their status, will usually command attention immediately.

If you feel you are none of the above you can easily find yourself resorting to more juvenile tactics to gain attention, like loud, guffawing laughter or a feverishly high level of gesticulation, or you may teeter into more dodgy territory, like dressing or behaving in a way that implies you are an easy lay. These tactics might get you noticed, but remember that you are trying to attract attention for the *right* reasons.

The first impression is a lot like a job interview. Your skills, your behaviour, your intellect and your personality might be subtle beyond belief, but most of these hidden depths will only emerge later, if you get the job. In the meantime you might put yourself out of the running by wearing the wrong tie or sitting in a funny way.

In this first-glance scenario you will need to create enough of the right sort of impact for the man/woman to whom you are attracted to feel the first few tentacles of mutual appeal, or, as a Mills and Boon novel might put it, 'the first stirrings of desire'. At this point your skills are going to have to be quite general, but it is relatively easy to double your chances of being thought attractive by using a few simple, quick-fit tricks which are described later in the chapter. Without these techniques you face the danger of becoming an 'instant deletion'.

Deletions

When we hunt for a mate at a social event we scan the room quickly for potential targets. Even when we are not actively on the prowl, or when we are in non-social situations, like the workplace, we are still scanning subconsciously.

One glance can be all it takes for us to achieve the first cull and disqualify those meriting instant deletion. These are people who seem too old, too young, too short or of the wrong sexual group and so on for our tastes. We will initially be aware of their presence and general non-sexual potential, but that is all. Women often complain that they feature permanently among the deleted as they get older. Many claim to feel that they have become all but invisible once their looks have faded.

Often, the older we are the less picky and more open-minded we may become, and more likely to be keen to go beyond first impressions, whether the other person is a fit with our mental specs or not. This may have less to do with new-found maturity and more to do with good old lack of choice. The older you get the more potential partners get snaffled by marriage or the Grim Reaper. Only the very young can afford to go through potential mates like the man from Del Monte picking through a crop of peaches.

To stand a chance with someone after being deleted at a social gathering you will have to infiltrate their consciousness more subtly, maybe waiting until they have had a couple of drinks – by which time their 'bottom line' as regards attractive qualities may have become distinctly more negotiable – and then finding a pretext to engage them in conversation, so that you can display more subtle attraction skills, like listening and flirting. Time is the crucial asset. If you can get talking to the person you like and then develop the transaction beyond first impressions you can then call on more complex skills to work your way onto their 'partnership potential' list.

The deleted are by no means all losers. You can be deleted from below as well as from above. Men or women who are *too* beautiful or successful or high-status may be rejected along with those who are too old, too young, too ugly or of the wrong sex. The other person will be seeking some sort of physical match. What they are also looking for, remember, is someone they believe will find *them* a match, too.

Getting Past First Base

To enhance your chances of a first-base hit, then, you'll need to work on the social attraction factors, making yourself look as good as possible, but in a way that is appropriate and relatively subtle. Over-signal (a red dress, acres of cleavage, glossy lips, big hair, or bulging pecs, tight jeans and a tight vest, and so on) and you could over-shoot the runway.

Work too on your instant character signals. Again, you can begin to signal something bordering on a global ideal. For instance, most people are attracted to positivity, friendliness, honesty and warmth.

Body to Body

To create 'first impression' attraction there will need to be a match of body behaviour – a physical empathy or rapport, a suggestion that you two could be the Torvill and Dean of the bedroom. Your body has its own rhythm of movement. This style of personal choreography will send unspoken signals to a potential mate, suggesting physical and sexual compatibility. The physical signals will be subtle but high-impact in the response they obtain. Combined with impressions of body shape, these signals will give your potential mate strong messages about your sexual compatibility.

At this stage your potential mate will be basing his/her assessment of your personality and sexuality on any or all of the following:

• Gaze

• Facial expression

• Posture

- Gestures

- Grooming

- Smell

- Dress

- Spatial behaviour

- Touch

These silent signals are essential for effective bonding. When it comes to dating and mating successfully, society has provided us with little alternative. To wander up to a man or woman at a party and drop your sexual preferences into the first few lines of conversation would generally be viewed as being a bit pushy. Letting that person know you are interested in them sexually at all takes subtlety unless you're very young and very drunk. Anyone adopting the moustache-twirling antics of a Leslie Phillips would immediately be dismissed as a lech.

You can improve your chances of attracting the right person by about 70 per cent if you study, improve and rehearse your body language and image techniques.

And the catch is?

Well, initially we're probably going to be limited to the more superficial stuff. Most of these signals are very, very subtle. But what we're going to do is develop a range of basic 'attention-and-attraction' skills.

Creating Instant Impact

1 Plan your outfit

Create instant rapport by dressing to suit the pack that he/she moves in. Remember that scene in *Grease*, when Olivia Newton-John emerges from the gingham and lace clad in Lycra pants and John Travolta's eyes pop out? There's no need for you to gear up like an identikit, but sport a similar image and you will seem an easier fit with his/her social group.

If the group is new to you and their fashion culture as yet unknown, do what you would do at a job interview: dress without making a strong statement. Avoid backing one horse until you've seen the field. No need to look overly bland, but shelve the pinstripes or the tie-dye until you're confident they will make the right impression.

2 Plan your entrance

Packs *always* turn to study a new arrival. It's part of the survival instinct. When you walk into that party or bar you will be noticed by nearly every person in the room, even if they don't appear to be looking. Prepare for a good entrance before you get to the door. Think about who you want to look like ('And tonight, Matthew, I am going to be ...'). Pull yourself up to your full height. Pull your shoulders back and down. Focus all your energy into the chest and shoulder area. Imagine that your feet are floating way off the ground. Raise your head enough to pull your chin taut, but never lift the chin to the point where it makes you look arrogant or aloof.

3 Kick out the old baggage

It is true that shit happens. The older you get, the more baggage you tend to collect. Broken romances, failed marriages, jiltings, turn-downs and let-downs affect everybody. But wearing these battle scars will only serve to decrease your chances of pulling someone new.

Imagine how you would feel if nothing bad had ever happened in your love life, if no one had ever dumped you or done the dirty on you. Now think how you would look. Your face would be open and smiling, no frowns or worry lines. You could look anyone straight in the eye and expect a positive response. You'd stand tall and you'd use open, positive gestures.

Now look at the picture you present in a full-length mirror. Every wrong in your life may be etched there on your body and the way it moves, betrayed by avoidance of eye contact, nervous smiles, closed, protective gestures, anxious comfort touches and fiddling.

Which image do you suppose is the more attractive to other people – that of the walking wounded or that of the confident, seemingly unscarred person?

As we get older the battle scars increase. Older people are

supposed to make more considerate, practised lovers and come free of the baggage of small kids and big debts, but they can sure be a pain in the arse when they bang on about all the times their hearts have been broken. If age is to teach us anything it should be to let the emotional baggage go and embrace relationships free of past misery. Dragging it with you makes establishing a good relationship difficult. When a first date ends with someone telling a friend 'We talked all night – I felt as though I could tell him/her anything', you just know that the person concerned has bored for Britain, offloading broken hearts, failed marriages and bastard behaviours.

4 Adopt role models

If the battle scars are difficult to erase, or your attempts to act more confident than you feel result only in a rictus smile and mad-dog eyes, you could always try a spot of personal cloning. As part of your preparation for an evening out, close your eyes and imagine who you would most like to look like at that moment. Who would handle the situation you are about to confront with style and courage? Who would be deemed attractive and memorable?

If you watch the TV programme *Stars in Their Eyes* you will know the formula: some humble, plain, bumbling little no-mark disappears behind a screen and re-emerges smiling and waving, through a cloud of mustard gas, in the style of their chosen celebrity. This is the type of transformation you will be undertaking, only without the aid of dry ice and a make-over department.

Imagine you have become your chosen person. How would they look and act? What kind of gestures would they use? How would they walk? What would their facial expression say? Charismatic celebrities aren't known for looking nervous or haunted when they walk into a room. Most of them carry themselves upright and smile. These are the traits you will be adopting. If you are shy you will find it easier to 'perform' in the style of someone else. Like putting on a mask, it can help you rid yourself of your inhibitions. Many actors are shy when they are being themselves, but are able to play someone else quite easily.

The added bonus of this strategy is that it will have a positive effect on your subconscious emotions. By *acting* more
confident you will begin to *feel* better, too. Body movements
have a strong effect on our moods and emotions, as you will
see in the chapter on confidence.

5 Imagine ...

Life has been good to you. You are always lucky in love. You
have never been jilted, hurt, insulted, stood up on a date,
divorced, and so on. Your kids have never insulted you or
called you mutton dressed as lamb. So ...

Take and release a deep breath. Raise your eyebrows slightly
and feel all the negative frown lines being ironed out of your
face.

Blink slowly and get rid of the fear and the wounded look in
your eyes. The slow blink is an effective attraction tool because
it can give a slow-mo effect to your appearance, and they
always use slow-mo in films when the hero first claps eyes on
the woman he is going to fall in love with. It implies the
moment is frozen in time. Think of this slow-mo effect and
replicate it in your body language. (Don't replicate slow-mo
walking or running, though, or you could end up looking more
Chariots of Fire than *Love Story*.)

Smile. Drop your hands – you don't need to use your arms as
comfort barriers. Feel full of energy, enthusiasm and optimism.

Imagine that the outfit you are wearing is Armani rather
than Next.

Imagine you are *always* lucky.

Imagine you are famous.

Imagine the party is waiting for you before it can start.

Imagine you are walking into a room full of your best
friends.

Then adjust your posture and facial expression accordingly.
Soften your eyes. That blank, worried stare will look grim
rather than suave. Walk into the room looking as though you
have just been told an amusing – but not belly-wobbling –
joke.

If you arrive alone, ask your host to introduce you to
someone interesting. If you arrive with friends, don't stand and

talk in a group. Go straight up to someone else in the room and introduce yourselves. People expect groups to be talking about things of common interest, and this makes them appear hard to penetrate.

Look around the room, but not while you are supposed to be listening to someone else talking. This can make you look rude and vain. Avoid preening gestures as you do so. Touching or flicking your hair will make you look arrogant and self-obsessed.

Avoid looking false while you are talking to others. Loud laughter and stretched 'social' smiles will make you seem insincere. Avoid comfort gestures. Don't fiddle with jewellery, your tie or your clothing. Don't touch your face.

If you are holding a drink, keep it just above or at waist height. If you are carrying a bag, don't clutch it hard to your body.

Look interested in the person who is speaking in your group.

Social Interaction

When we watch a potential mate for the first time we are keen to discover two things: how they relate to others – their social potential – and how they will relate to us.

We are happier if the two diverge – we want a different response to that offered to the rest of the room. So flirting with anyone and everyone in the room is not going to be perceived as charming and alluring. The impact of your flirting will only be positive if it is reserved for one person alone. Splatter-gun flirting is a weapon that's best kept for a moment when you have been turned down in some way. It's done to make someone in an existing or recently deceased relationship jealous, not to attract a new mate. Details of effective flirting techniques can be found later in the book.

All these tips will help make you look more attractive if you are being monitored. If you feel the person you want to attract has not noticed you, then get the host or hostess to introduce you. Never try to attract attention by loud or outrageous behaviour, and avoid especially the loud laugh. This affliction can affect men and women of any age. I should know – I have one myself. If you find it hard to get rid of, at least turn it into a more attractive feature. Elizabeth Taylor, for instance, has a wonderfully dirty giggle, which is completely at odds with her visual image and therefore charming.

'The Look'

Now – the big moment when you make eye contact with the person you like. If you are a man you can affect a longer, slightly bolder stare, as though smitten by this person's great beauty. A woman should glance for one second, then look away – but only for a bit! The trick is then to look back again, this time with a more meaningful glance and a slight smile. And if this sounds like sexist stereotyping, then feel free to go for the other role. It's up to you. I just don't see Clark Gable looking very pretty getting dimpled and coy over Scarlett O'Hara, that's all.

I don't expect this will come naturally to you, so it would be wise to give this key gesture a thorough work-out in the mirror first. It's not exactly industrial-strength flirting, but it is the first vital step in the dance. In fact, for God's sake *do* practise it first. I thought I was quite good at it at one time, until I checked in the mirror and discovered I was mimicking the expression Alan Rickman wears in his role as Professor Snape in the Harry Potter movies (very evil!).

Once you have attracted attention and made a connection, resist the temptation to inform your friends, because they will all turn to stare. Instead, concentrate on your posture. Stretch your spine by trying to touch the ceiling with the top of your head. Take and release a deep breath. Pull your stomach in, but without puffing out your chest. If you are a woman, arch your back very slightly and tilt your head back for a second, displaying your throat. (Yes, I know this throat and inside arm stuff is mentioned in every book on flirting, and I promise not to mention the soft white forearm flesh, but the small throat gesture works, I promise. Men think it looks polite but raunchy.)

Make sure you are participating in your group's conversation – don't look like a misfit. Be animated but remember that

you have just been mentally poleaxed by this love-god/
goddess you have just spotted. Glance back again. Smile. Make
it a secret-looking smile, with no teeth showing but lots of
eye-softening.

Don't eat unless you are supremely confident. Most of us
miss our mouths under pressure. Sip, don't gulp, your drink.

If you are a young man, resist the temptation to show off.
Don't flip beer mats or chuck peanuts into your mouth. Never
wrestle your friends. Girls think this sort of stuff is silly, not
heroic. (*Please*, resist these temptations if you are a more
mature man, too.)

Male or Female?

Are there set roles in this stage of the engagement? Do men
really have to do the looking and women the glancing away?

Well, those are the traditional roles. But they probably stem
from a time when women were more passive during sex, as
well. I've seen women stray heavily into Leslie Phillips territory, hitting on men in a manner that would make their
grandmothers reach for the eau de Cologne.

In a way the who-does-what debate is largely settled by the
who's-looking-for-what question. If a man is looking for a
more traditional women he'll probably fall for the blushing
young virgin routine. If a man prefers to be less dominant he
might equally be charmed by the woman taking the initiative.
Ditto for women. If you like your man to be the strong, silent
Heathcliff type you'll relish the impassioned stare while you
look away and then back again. If 'cute 'n' shy' is more your
thing, then you'll prefer the roles reversed.

Power Signals

The instantly held eye gaze shows that you have in some way
selected the recipient from out of the crowd. It sanctions a
move to the next stage – for one of the pair to move across to
speak. The signal is vital – it needs to be sent and returned,
otherwise the relationship may never get off the starting
blocks, especially if you are in a room full of relative strangers.

But this point in the proceedings will also involve power signals. Already one of you is being defined as the more dominant. The more aggressive the first approach – a wolf whistle, a wink, a leer – and the more submissive the response – blushing, looking away, giggling – the more firmly the lines of apparent status are drawn.

Instant Turn-offs

Yes, I did the survey. What body language turns you off most? I asked both men and women. The one thing both sexes had in common was their overwhelming enthusiasm to give me this information. They all thought for a moment, then they smiled, then the stuff started to pour out. If they paused at all it was only to gather momentum. Occasionally the smiles faded and real anger or disgust kicked in.

This is the body language women most hate in men:

- Crotch displays (sitting or standing with legs wide apart)

- Wedgie-hiking (scratching around the crack in your bottom, especially while you're talking)

- Picking at spots

- Crotch-fiddling. (It did nothing for Michael Jackson. It even did very little for Robbie Williams. Continentals do it. Footballers do it. It tends to look as if you have a rash or something sexually transmittable. *Not* a turn-on.)

- Leaning over a woman when you talk

- In an office situation, leaning back in your chair with your hands behind your head and your feet on the desk

- Talking while you eat

- A smug smile

- Jangling change in your pocket

- Peering over the top of sunglasses

- Putting sunglasses on the top of your head

- Fiddling with your hair constantly

- Compulsive leg-twitching

- Knuckle-cracking

- Throwing admiring glances at yourself in the mirror

- Throwing admiring glances at other women

- Sniffing

- Burping

This is what women do that turns men off:

- Acting like a man

- Possessive or grooming gestures – picking hairs off a jacket or dusting off dandruff – in front of others

- Continual tapping on the man's arm while talking

- Wearing a short skirt and then tugging the hem down all the time

- Standing with legs apart and hands on hips

- Arms constantly folded

- Arms flapping about

- Arms and legs crossed

- Hiking bra down

- Hanging about the bar looking blank while the drinks are being paid for

- Sarcastic smiles

- Yawning

- False-sounding laughs

- Nail-biting

- Displaying too much cleavage in a very obvious manner

So now you know. Disagree with any of the above points if you like, but remember – you can't argue with another person's feelings. Image and impact are non-negotiable. If you want to impress, stop doing any or all of the above.

The Next Steps

Once you have got past these first few vital stages you will be moving into deeper emotional and sexual negotiations. This is where your sex signals will become subtler and more specific. To understand these steps you will need a greater understanding of the body language processes. You will also need to firm up inner levels of confidence and self-esteem, because your signals and your ability to read those of others will have to extend beyond the superficial. This is why the next two chapters focus on bodytalk and confidence.

CHAPTER FOUR

Bodytalk: A Beginner's Guide

First, then, some basic explanations of a very complex set of competencies. Improving your bodytalk means understanding the signals you currently send and receive, discovering how to read others' signals more skilfully, and then taking charge of your own response.

Body language signals are as subtle and ritualistic as a Chinese opera. There are some movements and expressions that are innate, although scientists argue about exactly how many of our gestures would appear naturally, without our mimicking others, which is how we acquire most of our techniques. We see, we understand, we mirror, just as in verbal communication.

Generic Responses

Movements that are more instinctive than learned are called generic. Many of these reactive gestures and facial expressions have an evolutionary link. Most have been built around emotional responses or states, and all have an important role to play in our ability to survive. Surprise, for instance, is registered by the widening of the eyes, often known as 'eye-popping'. In fight-or-flight mode, this eye-widening would enable us to see more of what is going on around us. It is the perfect response to a new – and possibly threatening – stimulus.

A tight pursing of the mouth, a narrowing of the eyes and a shake of the head register disgust. The mouth-pursing makes eating impossible, so disgust at bad and potentially poisonous food protects us from consuming that food.

When we are angry our muscles tense, making the jaw look firmer and wider. The eyes narrow, making them less vulnerable, and the face reddens, which can be a frightening display for the onlooker. We put our hands on our hips and puff up our chests – the human equivalent of a bird fluffing out its feathers or a cat its fur, making it look like a bigger, tougher, more threatening opponent.

Your generic responses can affect your body language when you see someone you like. Facial features soften and you smile more, making you look more attractive. A man might puff his chest out, to make himself look stronger, while a woman tends to pout a little more and push her breasts out to look more sexual.

Learned Responses

Other body language signals have to be learned over time. When we use them we register what works and what doesn't – what behaviour is rewarded and what isn't. A smile might please the parent. A cry summons attention. A look of fear or upset will stimulate a desire to comfort and a cuddle. Children watch the bodytalk of adults and role-play it for themselves in the form of games. I recently watched a small girl mimic her mother with a toy mobile phone. She had the entire routine off pat, from the exasperated facial expressions to the pauses to the drag on an invisible cigarette. This little game made her mother laugh, but the child was carefully incorporating smoking and ill temper into its repertoire, probably for life.

Much of your sexual repertoire, then, will have been copied from parents, peers and conscious or subconscious role models. The success of these learned techniques will depend on whether or not the person you 'borrowed' them from was successful, and whether his or her gestures sit well on your frame. In a way this is a little like borrowing someone's clothes: a lot will depend on the fit.

Sexual Skills

As we progress through life we learn new body language skills. Some of these may be through copying others, but many are entirely new, many totally practical. You learn to ride a bike, and then drive a car. Your hands acquire keyboard skills or the capacity for more delicate work, like sewing or flossing your teeth.

Of necessity, most of your sexual bodytalk skills will have been picked up through trial and error as you go along. Otherwise it's down to watching raunchy scenes in movies, in which case you will need to remember that the people involved were acting, and they were trying not to mess up their hair.

The sexual rituals take us through all the body language skills. When you meet someone you find attractive, your displays will largely be dictated by an evolutionary response – an attempt to attract in quite a basic, animal, instinctive manner – with some copied behaviour that you might have learned from a parent or a peer or an admired celebrity. Then, when you get to the stage of the sex act itself, you will start to use more technical skills which may have taken years to perfect. (If this last statement has got you worried because you either haven't got to this stage or were unaware of its existence, don't worry unduly – there are plenty of manuals on the market to help you hone your techniques. Try Lou Paget, for a start: *How to Give Her Absolute Pleasure, How to Be a Great Lover* and *The Big O* – all published by Piatkus.)

So when we meet someone new, how do we go about reading and delivering all these intriguing body language signals?

Cluster Signals

When we meet someone, we evaluate what we see in a hugely complex process, making enormous assumptions based on prejudice and stereotype which involve an intriguing 'matching' operation. Imagine your brain to be a computer containing police files. If the police are looking for a criminal the computer goes through the files of thousands of villains until it comes up with potential matches, based on similarities in witness descriptions. Similarly your brain looks at gestures, expressions and physical appearance and 'matches' them to anything similar it might have come across before. Then it will tend to assume that this new person has all the same traits as the one it has matched him/her to.

Our eyes take in the visual signals and judge them by balancing one against the other to come up with an overall assessment. Some negatives may outweigh positives, or vice versa. For instance, arrogant signals might be balanced by some immature, childish displays that form an overall impression that the person is masking a lack of confidence or experience with a show of bravado.

We rarely judge on one gesture alone, which is why an assertion such as 'He touched his nose, which means he is lying' is patent tosh. However, individual signals are worth studying in isolation when you work on your own sexual repertoire, as it is easier to improve your signalling step by step rather than as a single entity.

If your signals look negative in any way, the chances are your new acquaintance will start to look for confirmation of his or her initial adverse reaction. We all like to kid ourselves that we are good at judging other people. So when we make a judgement we like to have it confirmed – we look for evidence to back up our first evaluation. This is what is known as a self-fulfilling prophecy.

Communication Breakdown

To analyse what happens during the process of communication, and how the brain turns body language into assumed knowledge, you need to understand the three major stages that transform gestures and expressions into an emotional response.

1 Stimulus
You frown, you smile, you fold your arms. This is the only stage of the communication that is largely non-negotiable. If I pointed my finger at you, you could stand up in court and give

evidence to the fact that I pointed which would have to be admissible. Everyone saw it, even me.

2 Assumption

Now we start to part company. Working from previous experience, you will begin – often subconsciously – to decide *why* I pointed. If you had a teacher who did it when she was telling you off, you might imagine I was being aggressive. If you had no negative memories you might think I was just trying to illustrate direction or gain your attention. No two life experiences are the same, therefore no two people will analyse the *why* in exactly the same way.

3 Assimilation and response

Now we really begin to tippy-toe down trash alley. If you disliked that teacher telling you off, you may find you begin to dislike me too. If, on the other hand, you found the teacher's telling-off somehow stimulating, the reverse might apply – you could even find yourself getting turned on by the strict approach.

Like, dislike, trust, wariness, distaste or attraction can all be strongly formed at this stage of the communication.

So which parts of your body are the 'noisiest' in non-verbal communication terms?

Posture

Life tends to etch itself on the spine. Like lines on the face, which linger as a constant echo of past emotions, the way your body tends to distribute its weight will tell others a lot about how your life has gone to date. Deep grooves around the mouth and across the forehead will suggest that you have spent much of your life frowning and unhappy. Similarly a slumped or low-gravity stance can imply low self-esteem or high levels of self-protection, suggesting past battles and tragedies. High-gravity posture, on the other hand, will tend to look positive and focused. (This will all be described in more detail later in the book.)

Eye Contact

I've mentioned the 'eyes meeting across a crowded room' scenario. Eye contact is one of the most high-impact communicators we have, the opening gambit in attraction and seduction. So much so that when I was interviewed on a radio programme for the blind and asked how blind people can tell who might fancy them at a party I was stumped for an answer.

Too much eye contact, though, as in a hard stare, may be interpreted as arrogant or aggressive. Too little may appear passive or negative.

Facial Expression

We have an impressive number of muscles in our faces, which are therefore capable of a whole raft of subtle and not-so-subtle signals. Even one small, flickering movement can create a very high-impact signal to another person. Micro-gestures are often facial. These dramatic expressions happen so quickly they are perceived only subliminally. To watch them properly you'd need to freeze-frame a camera shot. They are the moment your face creates an often involuntary expression that may well reveal hidden – and usually negative – emotions, such as dislike or even disgust.

Gestures

Leakage is a term that describes the way your body 'leaks' hidden feelings or emotions. Most leakage occurs from the hands or the feet, which are at the extremities of the body and are therefore the hardest to control. Leakage gestures include tapping, fiddling and chewing nails.

Illustrative gestures are useful because they paint a visual picture in the listener's mind. They come in the form of mime when you describe something.

Emphatic gestures are used to attach emotion to a word. They should appear natural and relatively spontaneous, rather than rehearsed or repetitive.

Denial gestures damage your message by diluting or negating it. You might tell someone you are interested in what they have to say while at the same time glancing at your watch. Or you might shrug when asked whether you are all right while replying verbally in the affirmative.

Signal gestures are used to make a controlled and specific communication, such as a thumbs-up to signal approval or a V-sign to suggest lack of it.

Distractive tics are spontaneous gestures that add little to your communication and rob it of much of its impact. You might flutter your hands or cartwheel your arms or make gurning expressions, owing to nerves or anxiety. In communication terms, these gestures lead to confusion.

Spatial Behaviour

The amount of space between you and another person is dictated by the relationship between you. Rules regarding social space are almost engraved in stone. It is the distance you would stand behind the next person in a bus queue, or where you would stand if you were making small talk at a party. The intimate zone is reserved for people we are comfortable touching and being touched by. When you meet a potential partner you may well move very swiftly from the social to the intimate zone. The speed at which you do so needs to be comfortable for both people, though. Unwelcome or uninvited touch is predatory.

When you start to touch a new or potential partner you should begin a game of move-and-monitor. By this I mean that you should try touching them and watch their response. Do they freeze up? Are there any symptoms of embarrassment, like giggling or looking away? Do they offer the next touch, or is it left up to you?

This is a ritual you may play throughout the relationship, even after sex has taken place. Everyone has a different set of personal rules about touch. Some sexually involved couples never touch in public. Others are more openly tactile. Many men prefer to keep touch within the sexual ritual, while many women say that they would sometimes just like to be cuddled in a non-sexual scenario.

Patterns of Behaviour

So why do you do what you do?

Your entire current repertoire of attraction techniques is based on what is called rewarded behaviour – in other words, it has worked at some time in the past. The problem is that that was then and this is now. What worked on one person might be a turn-off for another. And most of your 'reward' techniques were established so long ago it was sweets you were after, not sex.

While most patterns of emotion and behaviour are more complex than fine lace, the rewarded behaviours, the emotions and responses that have got us what we want in life, are as simple as a piece of thick string. If a baby cries and gets fed, then it sees no reason to change this simple strategy, because it obviously works like a dream. Unless there appears to be some flaw in the plan, that 'baby' will still be turning on the water-works as a manipulative technique well into middle age.

The same is true of our attempts to be liked or loved by others. We see someone we want and all the old trace patterns kick in our desire to make ourselves attractive to them. Hopefully we will be having the same effect on this other person. But attraction isn't always instant for both parties. If your current patterns of behaviour aren't working, or aren't working in the way you want them to, then it must be time for a change.

Focusing on the Present

Before you start to focus on changing your behaviour to appeal more to others during the early stages of meeting, you need to be aware of the current reality, what it is that you tend to do at present.

Take some paper and write two lists. Ask yourself: When I see someone I like, what tactics do I use to a) get his/her attention, and b) be instantly appealing? How do you make yourself noticeable? Or do you tend to become invisible through shyness or nerves? Do you gesticulate more and get louder? Do you become more animated and laugh a lot? Do you blush? Do you show off? Do you begin to tease, joke with and even insult the person you like? Do you go quiet?

And how do you flirt?

See yourself in action. Close your eyes and remember past incidents, then move into the future. Imagine yourself moving in on someone you find attractive. Imagine any of a number of scenarios, if it helps. See yourself at work, at a party, in a club or bar, and so on.

Then ask yourself: How comfortable do I feel in these situations? How easy do I find it to attract someone and then flirt with them? Do I think my techniques are effective, or could they be improved? How long have I been using these techniques? Or do I just go with the flow and hope I can do my best?

Do I feel my attraction techniques are helping or hindering my ability to attract a mate? Who did I learn/copy them from? Are they working or not? What do I need to change?

Changing Your Behaviour

To modify your own body language you'll need to start changing a few old habits. This is probably easier than you think. According to most psychologists, an old habit can be changed in as little as 21 days. A new habit can be learned a lot faster. Think how long it took for you to learn to drive a car. Remember how many lessons it required before you were changing gear without thinking about it consciously. That was the moment you consigned the skill to 'muscle memory', when your body became able to bypass conscious thought processes and move involuntarily. The human body is a wonderful exception to the adage about teaching old dogs new tricks. It is one old dog which actively enjoys learning new tricks, and will do so easily, if you let it. The only barriers will be embarrassment, mild discomfort and negative thinking.

Comfort Zones

When you learn a new skill you get knocked – temporarily – outside your comfort zone. You feel awkward at first, and the temptation is to return to that comfort zone – to go back to doing what you've always done. But remember: *If you always do what you've always done then you'll always get what you've always got.*

Sound about right? By stepping outside your existing skill zone and advancing to a new grade you get to achieve things that were never possible before. In terms of the theme of this book, you will be making yourself more attractive to potential partners. You are learning how to read their signals more effectively and understand the silent communications of sex, remember? That's worth a little initial awkwardness, surely?

Do versus Don't

To change your body language you need to focus on the do's, not the don't's. Telling yourself what *not* to do will only have the opposite effect. The brain tends to delete the word 'don't' from any self-command. So coach yourself through change by means of 'do' messages. See how you want to move and behave. Visualise the new, more attractive, confident, positive you. Think man-magnet or babe-magnet. See the changes working.

If you have difficulty visualising perfection, you can always try a spot of plagiarism.

Studying Role Models

Make a list of those you see as having a strong social and 'instant' appeal, who are immediately attractive to a wide range of people. The list can include the famous and the non-famous. They need to be people who are 'special', though; the type you could quite confidently predict most – if not everyone – you know would find attractive in some way.

Now look at the list and see whether you can establish what it is they have in common. To acquire a skill you first need to discover what it is. Never be worried about copying talent. Plagiarism is the first rule of a successful image. You do what you do because you copied your parents; now it's time to start copying people who are the leaders in their field. What makes their appeal so strong? Is it *just* their beauty, or is it something else as well? Is it qualities like confidence and self-esteem? How many people on your list are not beautiful in the regular sense? What is it they do that makes them attractive? What is it in their performance that you can start to copy?

Now begin to refine the process. For instance, if you have written 'Confidence' down on your list, write down alongside it how that quality exists in physical terms. What did those people *do* to make you believe they were confident? Was it a smile? Or the way they held themselves? Beauty comes from the shape or the line. *Attraction*, however, tends to be self-created. It's what we *do* with the body shape we have been given. What do these people you have deemed to be attractive *do* with their body shapes?

Upgrading Your Competence

These are the stages involved in the process of learning a new skill like body language:

1 Unconscious incompetence

You begin in a state of relative unawareness. Your body language is instinctive. When you get to see yourself on video, though, you scream and recoil in horror, which takes you to stage two:

2 Conscious incompetence

You become aware that your bodytalk is letting you down. When you meet someone you fancy you become a clone of Mr Bean. You also get confused when trying to understand your potential partner. You feel you could do better with both the outgoing and incoming signals, so you move to stage three:

3 Conscious improvement

You begin to change your body language to make it more effective. Only you feel awkward as a result. Your body tells you to nip back to stage one again. At least you felt all right there, even if you didn't look it. But persevere – waiting in the wings is stage four:

4 Unconscious improvement

You modify your own signals and you stick with them through the awkward stages. Suddenly you're better all the time, but without too much effort. You've stopped folding your arms and biting your top lip when you get nervous with someone you like. Your smile is more natural and you're able to use wonderfully seductive eye contact. The discomfort starts to fade as muscle memory kicks in. Now all you have to do is start beating them off with a stick …

Remember:

- Don't waste energy envying others. See whether they have any tricks you can copy. 'Luck' usually only results from a lot of hard work.

- Be prepared to step outside your comfort zone in an effort to improve.

- Be focused on your goals. You can achieve much, much more than you think.

- Plan first, but never put off action. Sitting at home by yourself is no way to assess how attractive you are to others. Get out there and start networking.

- Accept no sick notes from yourself. Lame excuses for poor performance or 'no-shows' are simply not acceptable. When you start to excuse yourself before you've even tried you have started to make failure a friend. Ask yourself: 'Am I *trying* to fail?' Never try a technique or theory just to prove it doesn't work.

How to Say No

What if you're on the receiving end of signals that you're not keen to reciprocate? How do you rebuff an unwanted pass early without causing offence?

You'd think it would be easy to signal 'no way, José' at the beginning of the game. Unfortunately lines of communication get crossed and gestures are misread. To the devout sexual optimist there is no such thing as a man/woman who will say no, just some that need a bit more pushing.

The process is a painful one because some initial flirt signals can be misleading. Shyness can look horribly like a lack of interest, as all shy people know to their disadvantage when the man/woman of their dreams comes over to talk and they find that they can neither speak nor move properly. I have seen countless TV programmes in which very young teenagers get to meet their pop idols. The kids will have been dying to meet this celeb, possibly for years, but, when the big moment comes, they can't move or even look at the star. Their body language signals could be mistaken for utter indifference. Many of us never grow out of these bursts of crippling shyness when we first see someone we like.

The simplest way to signal 'no' across a room, though, is just to turn your back. Don't look round again, even to see whether the person still has their eye on you. If you do, you might appear to be signalling interest, or at least to be participating in the first stages of the gaze ritual. Create a 'barrier' gesture by, for example, folding an arm across your chest. Lean in towards the person you are currently speaking to. If you are sitting down, break off any empathy signals by crossing your legs away from the interested party. Avoid any grooming gestures or body touches. Maintain your normal behaviour but avoid anything attention-seeking, like a loud laugh.

If you yourself receive any of these closed-down responses, take the signals as a 'no'. Don't try to move on to the next stages in the hope that you have misread them.

Incidentally, none of the above advice is aimed at getting rid of a sex pest. The best tactic with these people is to tell them that you are not interested and to take even more direct action if this verbal message is ignored. These more dainty rituals are intended to signal lack of interest in a social situation.

Mixed Messages

Always remember that social or business situations create a host of opportunities for mixed messages. Someone may be chatting to you because it is the polite thing to do, and not because they are lusting after your body. In the workplace the rules of engagement become even more complicated. Status enters into the equation. I've seen a lot of male bosses mistaking their PA's apparent adoration and willingness to say 'yes' to any question or demand for sexual attraction. It is very difficult to tell whether someone is really attracted to you when you are the boss.

It is also very hard for an employee to deal assertively with a sexual advance from their boss. Many will think their job is at stake. There are laws about these things, but often only one person in the scenario will try to play by the rules. Be *very* careful how you decipher the signals. Even when the person you like is a colleague, taking any rapport or flirting one step farther can be fraught with danger.

Acting the Part

Keep in mind the fact that a lot of what you are going to learn in this book could be described as acting or – in bodytalk terms – masking. I'm probably right in assuming you are not an accomplished thespian, though. Even if you were, you might still have a struggle with your body language.

It helps to start the improvement from within. Which means that the next step is to start working up a little confidence and self-esteem.

CHAPTER FIVE

Self-confidence: Building Attractiveness from the Inside Out

Remember that the way you *think* affects the way you *feel*, which affects the way you *act*, which in turn affects the way you *think*, and so on. Change one step in this loop and the other two will improve.

It's impossible to make your external signals perfect if the internal messages are flawed. OK, you may be a good actor, but even RADA-trained thesps have trouble making *every* movement convincing when they're treading the boards.

In body language terms acting is called masking. When you pretend to be more confident than you feel inside it is possible to keep up a good front, but only for short periods of time. Sooner or later your body gestures are going to suffer from what's called *leakage*, which means your true inner feelings start to leak out faster than lies from a politician's mouth.

You wear your internal feelings externally, like a sandwich board advertising your personality. When you are put under pressure – when you feel nervous or awkward during the first stages of a relationship – the slogan often starts to get more honest and revealing. You may waltz into a party wearing 'Charismatic and Delightful, with just a Hint of Rampant Sexuality' painted as your slogan back and front, but after a while you will probably be clad in 'Overweight Loser who Suffers from Shyness and Is Excruciatingly Boring'. Such is life.

The first person you need to sell yourself to, then, is *you*. Self-confidence can be bought in the guise of expensive clothes and grooming products, but if you lack inner self-esteem you need to start working from scratch.

Sexual Confidence

Are men more confident than women? According to men, no. I am constantly being reminded that men feel just as anxious and shy and nervous as women, although probably they are better at masking their insecurities. Women are more comfortable discussing their lack of self-belief. It is only in business that we have had to become accomplished bullshitters. Men, though, have to hone this skill from childhood. The ultimate 'test' for a man is his ability to get and maintain an erection. A lack of confidence can put this simple skill in jeopardy. The act of 'bluff' can be vital, then. In a way it is a form of self-coaching – convincing themselves that, despite the odds telling them that women like men who look like Tom Cruise and Brad Pitt, their own form of mongrel diversity from this ideal will somehow have some appeal.

The armour may be tougher, then, but the sensitivity is roughly equal. As women get older they seem to exert more pressure on one another about good looks than men do on them. Men will take the mickey out of one another as their waistlines grow and their hair disappears, but the overall bonding seems stronger. Groups of ugly-bug men will happily reaffirm one another's conviction that they can pull.

When I researched my book *Sex at Work* I was constantly amazed by the way packs of middle-aged, chubby businessmen spoke about one another as though they were young-buck Lotharios. What women saw as father and grandfather figures were seen by their colleagues as rampant sex gods, roaming the plains in search of the younger women in the firm and virtually taking their pick.

Self-esteem is a dominant factor in sexual attraction. Once you start to like yourself and the way you look you will find you give others permission to like you as well. If you are constantly sending physical and verbal messages saying that you're not up to much then you are guiding their perceptions and opinions of you in a negative direction. People who don't like themselves are hard to like. Confidence is contagious. But remember that confidence is not the same as arrogance. While confidence can be a turn-on, arrogance is predominantly a turn-*off*.

Creating Inner Confidence

Of course, this sounds easy, which it isn't. But don't let that put you off. Confidence is a great attractor. We are drawn towards confident people. They look better and appear easier to talk to. When that person is also charismatic, that confidence and positivity will seem contagious. They will make you feel better. Nelson Mandela spoke about 'allowing yourself to shine, because when you do you give those around you permission to do the same'.

So, *allow yourself to shine.*

A Personal MOT

Take a few minutes to assess your own thinking and the link with your behaviour patterns. Successful people tend to be focused and full of positive energy. That way they can spot good potential and power their way towards it. They think positively and act with purpose. If you can't emulate them you may tend to dither or be distracted from your goals.

Ask yourself whether you are:

1 High-energy and high-focus
If so you will find self-improvement relatively easy. You can identify your goals and devote energy to achieving them.

2 High-energy and low-focus
If this is you then you will be easily distracted. You find taking action quite easy but tend to waste all your energy on unplanned or unfinished projects.

3 High-focus and low-energy
You spend a lot of time thinking, planning, wishing and moaning, but very little on the 'doing' word. People may see you as rather remote.

4 Low-energy and low-focus

You will be seen as either very laid-back, to the point of torpor, or very negative. You have a tendency to dismiss or belittle the achievements of others, too. You tend to think they only succeeded because they were born lucky or lied about their success. Thinking like this justifies your own lack of effort.

Learning to Like Yourself

If you don't like yourself or the way you look very much you will have trouble understanding why anyone else might. Which means you may dislike or distrust anyone who tries to get closer to you.

How do you learn to like yourself?

Do some things that are admirable. List things you have already done that are brave or worthy or clever or good. Gain your own respect. Be assertive. Pinpoint areas of your life where you are acting like a doormat and do something about it. Be strong a couple of times a day. Do something nice for someone else, too – a favour without the expectation of anything in return.

And above all: *quit moaning.*

Moaning affects every fibre of your body. It is an ugly-making behaviour. It changes your posture and your facial expression and – as a consequence – hangs over you like a cloud of nuclear waste. Am I getting hysterical about this? You bet. Stop it. Stop it now.

Trying to Fail

Keep working the confidence 'muscle' and it will grow bigger and stronger. But you can also allow it to waste away by telling yourself and others that you are no good at things, unattractive, etc., or by creating mental 'sick notes' – excuses for not trying something, or not being good at it. Sick notes mean you are *trying to fail*. A typical sick note would be not chatting to the man/woman you fancy at a party because you just *know* they wouldn't find you attractive. Or not going to that singles evening because you're never good at that sort of thing.

The 'trying to fail' mentality is a tough act to beat. It's as though the future has already been written and it has 'don't bother' scrawled all over it. The good thing about the future is that we never know what it is going to hold. The only way you can possibly make predictions is when you start writing sick notes.

For instance, I *know* I will never win the lottery. The reason I know is I never buy a ticket. And why don't I buy a ticket? Because I'm never lucky with that sort of thing. How do I know that? Because I never win anything. Why do I never win anything? Because I never buy a ticket ... Do I need to go on, or do you get the message?

When I work with people who are 'trying to fail' I find I can cajole or bully them into trying a more positive, helpful technique, but they will only try it to prove me wrong. For them the satisfaction comes from proving it wouldn't work.

When you work on your body language techniques, never 'try to fail'. Give it your best shot and then keep on trying if it doesn't work first time.

Setting Confidence Targets

A good way to build confidence is to use the same techniques I use to overcome phobias. When we lack confidence in a situation we will often try to avoid it. It is tempting to stay within the comfort zone, even if life there is not getting us what we want.

There are situations in life that make us feel queasy. Many of them are social or 'performance' situations, like 'doing a room' at a party or getting up to make a speech. The only way to feel more confident about these situations is to get stuck in and do them. Work to improve your skills or techniques and then get going. The more often you try the easier it feels. Pursue the greater challenge and the smaller ones diminish.

If you only drove a car twice a year you would be a lousy driver. Skills improve with practice. The same applies to most things, from introducing yourself socially and making small talk to having sex. The more you do it the better you'll get. You won't be wonderful every time, but at least you will start to learn what works and what doesn't.

If you don't hit your target every time you should never end up thinking that your mistake was in trying at all. That's losers' talk and deserves a smack on the back of the legs. What you have learnt is what didn't work. That is only a technique problem, not a signal to give up. Sometimes we all need to recognise the point when we need to quit, but that point should never come before we even start to try.

I want you to jot down a page of 'Confidence Challenges'. These will be events that are not remotely life threatening or physically dangerous, but which will stretch you in terms of self-confidence. Think of occasions that make you go weak at the knees and note them down. They can be small-fry ('Trying to make small talk with a snooty-looking shop assistant') or big-bugger ('Making a speech at a friend's wedding', 'Making small talk to my demonic boss in the lift'). For me a small-fry would be making a bid at an auction or telling a joke to a social group, while big-bugger would be singing karaoke in a pub.

Face Your Greatest Fear

For most of us any test of inner confidence would include one all-time challenge, and it is this which you are going to have to come to terms with if you are going to grow and shine. The one great fear that most of us have is easily described. It is: THE FEAR OF LOOKING STUPID. THE FEAR OF MAKING A FOOL OF OURSELVES. THE INANE TERROR THAT WE MIGHT REVEAL OURSELVES TO OTHERS AS A STONKING GREAT PRAT.

Once you have recognised this and admitted it to yourself you can begin to deal with it. We are going to dissect this fear and – in doing so – overcome it. We are going to spank its little botty and send it off screaming for its mummy. It can only harm us if we allow it to.

The Idiot Factor

Being shown up as an idiot will neither kill you nor cause you physical harm. I am frightened of rock-climbing and playing

Russian roulette but I am not frightened of making a fool of myself. I have done it too many times. I even do it deliberately. A lot of the time I enjoy doing it. It makes people laugh. Clowns and comedians make fools of themselves for a living. The rest of the world is in some form of denial. We get too prissy. We are taught to act in a manner that the rest of society finds acceptable and that involves being serious and well behaved.

The worst thing I could be guilty of as a small child was 'showing off'. The other was 'acting stupid'. Playing the fool doesn't mean being stupid, though. Billy Connolly plays the fool but he is also a very intelligent man.

Think of a time in your childhood when you were taught to stop doing something because it looked childish or stupid. I was told this about sucking my thumb. For other children it was asking the question 'why?'. My generation was catapulted through childhood to the point where I was wearing make-up and heels by the age of eleven.

The fear of looking or sounding a fool is a very great inhibitor. Shy people fear it to the point where they would rather say or do nothing than end up being mocked. They collect memories of incidents in childhood when they were laughed at or teased and on the basis of these have decided that it's better not to try again.

When we fear ridicule we over-analyse every statement we make and find it wanting in the eyes of others before we have even uttered it. We imagine disapproval or mocking – so effectively that we see them even when they're not there.

I want you to lose this fear. It will inhibit every stage in the sexual process. Self-embarrassment is not going into the hand luggage on this particular journey. I once read about a man who trains actors in the skill of comedy. He said they find the training tough because they have to act the clown and this can make some of them aggressive. Fear emerges in many ways and aggression is just one of them. I'm going to ask you to do one important thing. To make you remember it I've worded it in a yucky way – but hey, who cares about looking stupid, right? I want you to:

Awaken the Clown Within

Sound familiar? OK, I pinched the idea. But it works when you want to boost your confidence. It is the first and most important step you can take. I worked as a catwalk model, and catwalk models are accident prone. Clothing falls off, heels snap, you trip over. What I learned, though, was not that humiliation in front of an audience is guaranteed, but rather that the audience only laugh *at* you if you are pompous and aloof. If you act like a nice human being they laugh *with* you. You *both* enjoy the laugh. The best sound for me is an audience laughing at my jokes. To get to that stage you need to let go of some of your life inhibitions. Inhibitions never make for a good sex life.

There are worse things in life than looking a little foolish. One is looking so aloof and cool that you never even get to speak to the person you like. Another is worrying so much about the way you look and sound that you end up saying and doing nothing. Life is full of risks. Risking your dignity on a very temporary basis is one of the smaller risks you can take.

Self-motivate, Self-coach

Remember one message: *Never be feeble.*

Be hard on yourself. Talk yourself up. Praise yourself. Tell yourself you look good. Tell yourself you *are* good. And repeat it.

Create personal mantras for key moments, like going into a party or approaching someone you like the look of. Tell yourself you like yourself. Tell yourself you like the way you look.

Personal mantras must sound good in your own ears, so I can't write them for you. Keep them simple, though. Examples might be:

• I feel calm, confident and in control.

• I look and feel beautiful.

• I ooze charisma.

• People are longing to meet me.

• I am funny, clever and sexy.

• I will allow myself to shine.

If any of these mantras sound laughably arrogant, don't worry. We're working on turning around decades of modesty and verbal self-abuse, so any shove in the opposite direction will need to be radical.

Relax and Grow

Each time you repeat your personal mantra, allow your body to relax and grow with the message. Feel the truth of the words and let them fill your body. The effect on your posture and body language will be massive, but not if you allow your cynical 'I feel stupid' voice to butt in.

To boost your self-confidence and self-esteem you'll need to begin to admire your appearance as well as your personality. The way you look will have had a tremendous effect on your inner self-esteem, and your self-esteem will have a tremendous effect on the way you look.

If you are young you will probably be using friends or fellow school or college students as a template for 'ideal' good looks. Girls, in particular, will have ways of judging who in their group is the most beautiful. Every school has its 'prettiest girl' and – surprisingly – their status is often unquestioningly accepted by others. They are admired and are even a source of pride. Interestingly, though, they are rarely the one the boys approach. That honour will go to the girl who is deemed the most *attractive*. This quality can be a huge mystery to the other girls, as they are less able to judge the relevant factors. They may be judging in terms of, say, slimness while the boys may be attracted to a curvaceousness the girls would consider fat.

Boys are probably even more baffled by the qualities required to be attractive to girls. Their role models are fewer and mainly attract the admiration of other boys, not girls. Confidence or cockiness is usually seen as the main attractor, as long as it is accompanied by a reasonable physique and facial good looks, although standards are far more variable. The simple truth is that the cocky boy is more likely to make the moves on the girls. This is where the lottery principle applies. They chat up several and pull one or two. The other boys see the win, but fail to notice the losses en route. Better-looking boys might avoid the risk of refusal by not trying in the first place, so the boy who does act and occasionally succeeds is seen as a champion.

Body Problems

How confident are *you* about your body? Do you like your shape? Or do you wish you were thinner/taller/more muscular? Are there parts of your body that you'd single out for improvement in an ideal world? Do you hanker after plastic surgery or a diet that works?

Physical fitness, by which I mean body self-approval, is vital if you want to appear attractive to a potential partner. Being happy in your own skin is the best way I can describe the physical confidence that I am trying to instil in you. It is a state in which you are making no verbal or non-verbal apologies for your looks. Not even in the form of jokes. I love humour, but most jokes are a form of aggression. When you take the mickey out of your appearance you are being aggressive towards yourself. This will start to sap your inner confidence. And God knows we need as much of that inner confidence as we can get, especially when we are on the pull.

To look good you have to display your physical strengths, not your weaknesses. When we acquire a hang-up about or dislike of a certain aspect of our appearance, we tend to emphasise it in two ways. First, we draw attention to it by talking about it. Strange, isn't it? Lack of self-esteem seems to force us to point out the very thing we hope will go unnoticed, and then keep referring to it. The reason offered for this odd behaviour is usually: 'I thought I'd bring it up before anyone else did.' The *real* reason, though, is often a psychological desire for approval. Mention your hulking great nose and you're sure to get someone to tell you it's petite and pretty. The self-insult is a manipulative trick to obtain a compliment and thus boost our ego. Only we know deep down that the compliment is merely flattery, and so we are compelled to repeat the process to the point of boredom.

Second, we draw attention to it by trying to hide or camouflage it. To try to divert eyes away from certain body parts we often cover them with our hands and/or arms. This makes them visually intriguing, which in turn makes them the focus of attention. The fact that you are telling other people not to look because these features are unattractive makes a statement that is hard to challenge. Other people usually agree with our self-assessment. If someone tells you they are boring or shy you will rarely tell yourself otherwise. If someone silently tells you not to look at his or her ugly mouth you will feel drawn both to look and to be repelled.

These acts of bodily downgrading will affect others' opinions of your looks, as well as your *own* opinions. Negative gestures are affirmation messages to your subconscious. Positive gestures improve your feelings of self-worth.

Body Check

Ask yourself, then: Which parts of my body do I dislike? Are there any concealment gestures I use with regard to those body parts? Do I cover my mouth with my hands when I laugh? Do I touch my nose as I talk? Am I constantly adjusting my hair? Do I cross my arms over my chest or stomach?

Any such concealment gestures will have to be eliminated from your repertoire. It's said that when the police ask a dealer where their drugs are hidden the dealer will always glance straight at the hiding place before answering with a lie. It's as though the body is desperate to tell the truth. Never allow your body to reveal all about any physical shortcoming. Always strive to look proud of the body you own, not ashamed of it.

Gussied Up

When you want to attract others you will probably do a lot to make yourself look your best. You might change your hair colour and style, use make-up or grooming products, and marinate yourself in colognes, deodorants and body sprays in an attempt to smell good, too.

Beauty and fashion products are great, but not if they create a state of self-negativity in your subconscious. When you use them, tell yourself that these products are for fun, but that you look even better without them. Otherwise they become a prop or a mask that you can't perform without.

Changing Your Inner State

If you learn to move in a confident manner then that physical state will create a positive affirmation for your subconscious – you will start to *feel* more confident as a result. Confident body language is relatively easy to learn, and I describe many of the gesture techniques throughout this book. A simple way to begin would be to:

- Stand to your full height.

- Roll your shoulders to release muscle tension.

- Push your shoulders back and down.

- Stretch your neck.

- Use open gestures – avoid shoving hands in pockets or folding your arms.

- Use emphatic gestures as you speak.

- Avoid fiddling or flapping gestures.

- Use prolonged bouts of eye contact, but soften the eyes into an 'eye smile' to avoid the appearance of staring.

- Breathe out to decrease tension in the torso. Make this out-breath last as long as possible. (If you feel the need to breathe in first to ensure you don't die of lack of oxygen, then go right ahead.)

- Smile.

These, then, are the six stages of confidence:

1. Stop trying to fail.
2. Stop worrying about looking stupid.

3. Start talking yourself up with positive mantras.
4. Keep working the confidence muscle – do daily confidence-boosting tasks.
5. Allow your inner confidence to grow into your body language.
6. Allow your body language to look more confident, to alter your mental state.

CHAPTER SIX

Location, Location, Location

OK, you've learned the basic skills of bodytalk and the impact of the first glance, and you've revved up your confidence levels. The next stage is to start learning a few tricks of flirting and charismatic character display. But before you start practising your industrial-strength eyelash-batting, there's something else to take into consideration.

What will you choose as your sexual hunting ground? This decision can be vital. The success of your first-step body language skills will be *heavily* dependent on *where* you intend to go to meet your prospective partner. Some locations encourage virtually instantaneous, fast-track meet-and-mate techniques, where you will have little opportunity to impress through intellect or depth of personality. Others will create time for manoeuvre into any or all of the later stages of chat-up.

The Mr Rochester Scenario

Remember Jane Eyre? Now in reality Jane would have had as much chance of pulling Mr Rochester as the Brooke Bond chimp has of pulling Jude Law. At one end of the scale put a powerful, loaded, moody, ugly-attractive (supposedly single) man complete with adorable ward and a large stately home, and at the other stick a sickly-looking, ugly little spinster who is determinedly down-dressed, and whose personality could only be described as shy, humourless and stubborn, and you would hardly expect the sparks to fly. This is a man whose first choice of wife was beautiful, exotic and barking mad, so where would you expect him to be looking next? Well, most probably in a similar direction, if his sexual inclinations moved him that way once. A man with a Jennifer Lopez poster on his wall is hardly going to be turned on by the Singing Nun, now, is he?

What Jane had on her side, though, was time. She lived in the guy's house. She was always there when he got home and fancied a bit of a chat. If they'd met at a dance she'd never even have got talking to him, let alone had the opportunity to give him a bit of lip. As far as her boss was concerned, she would probably have been one of life's deletions, on the grounds of age, social standing and class – and the Barbie factor.

But proximity created opportunity. Mr Rochester started to see beyond the mousy façade and discover the feisty, fiery sex-bomb that lurked inside. To add to his and Jane's luck, he also went blind. Unfettered by her determinedly drab appearance, he could focus on the spirited soul he had uncovered and imagine she looked like his first wife instead of Mother Teresa.

Play to Your Strengths

If you have control over your choice of hunting ground, always remember to play to your strengths. If you rate high on the social attraction monitor, then head for crowded spots like nightclubs, where you can turn heads quickly. If you are *too* good looking, though (I know, I know, some of us have this unsavoury cross to bear), keep in mind the like-attracts-like theory. People tend to be attracted to others at their own level. If you seem at a pretty unobtainable level, you may find you are deemed to be unapproachable, apart from by the most arrogant types, or those who know they compensate for lack of looks with something like power and/or status. If this latter type appeals to you, make sure you pitch up at a venue that is stocked with powerful/wealthy people, otherwise you're stuffed.

Although this book will tell you how to increase your chances of success wherever you meet your prospective partner, a little forward planning to select the best venue in which to play to your current image strengths would be useful. As a rough guide:

1 The club or bar

Pros: Dingy lighting will be flattering. Loud music can disguise a lack of personality.

Even in modern society, there is a fashion for hunting for your mate in dimly lit areas, like clubs and bars. Here you are 'allowed' to stare at the dancers, although the darkness tends to blunt many of your visual receptors, while the alcohol consumed makes you less critical. The idea of roamin' in the gloamin' is that you have a greater chance of appearing visually attractive if vision is deliberately impaired. Then verbal communication is rendered redundant by the volume of the music. All that's left is the sense of smell and some curious body language displays called dancing. No wonder people go out to clubs reeking of colognes, deodorants and aftershave. Get that element wrong and you're down to wiggling your bum to Kylie Minogue and praying for a result.

Cons: Emphasis is on looks and dress, so high social attractors tend to score best, although the darkness factor might be helpful if you rate low on the social attractor scale. Very little character development potential, with conversation limited beyond: 'D'you want a drink?' 'Yes, please, a Bacardi Breezer.'

Body language potential: Great potential for improving your chances. With communication reduced virtually to mime skills, the good mover can learn to excel, although only on the back of some initial visual profile fits.

The other challenge for the clubber is the ability to dance. When this is on the menu the whole concept of display behaviour reverts to something rather tribal. Women will still often use the dance floor as an opportunity to display body movement, shape and sense of timing and rhythm. Men still tend to watch before joining in. I know that dancing round the handbags is a relative cliché, but it still goes on in the less cutting-edge establishments, believe me. Current display styles include overt, bend-over bum-wiggling or arms-in-the-air stretching. Neither of these styles is easy for a bloke to join in with, so the purpose is mainly attraction.

When your grandparents sailed around the dance floor they were less into buttock displays and more into the foxtrot. This type of dancing was about partnerships, rather than being designed for solo display. To attract a male the women had to sit or stand about looking good. It was when the dancing started that the mating process began. All that ballroom stuff may have looked prim, but the effect was bodies pressed together in choreographed movement.

Real clubbers eschew the sexual-arousal stuff for arm-waving, pogo-style, high-energy displays. These might look non-sensual but they tend to occur in extremely crowded conditions. The waving and jumping will become a display of attention-seeking in difficult circumstances, and the more energetic the behaviour the higher the perceived status or confidence of the dancer. Drugs will also play a part here. The least inhibited can look like the most drugged up and therefore the most daring, wild or even hard.

Your ability to attract at these venues might depend on your style of physical movement, then, as well as your appearance. If you rate low on these two, don't lose all hope, though. I mentioned that we tend to attract our own level in terms of looks. The room won't always be full of good lookers who dance like Travolta. For every ugly-bug with two left feet there might be a corresponding partner watching and about to connect.

2 The dinner party
Pros: Hopefully flattering candlelight, but don't bank on it. Most DPs give you at least three hours in which to display your charms.

Cons: You could end up in the kitchen, under a strip-light, washing up.

Many hosts have a hideous frenzied desire to 'make up numbers'. This means there will only be the two of you spare, while the rest are what Bridget Jones called 'Smug Marrieds'. They will spend the evening watching like hawks to see whether either of you offer the other a lift home or not. The pressure of performing to others can lead to you being ignored totally.

Body language potential: Heaps of ways to enhance your performance, unless they stick the candelabra between you. The main problem is that you will feel yourself under scrutiny from well-meaning friends, plus they might keep offering verbal prompts, like: 'Tell Fred about the time you got trapped in the greenhouse ...'

Be polite and charming and employ listening body language. Avoid overt displays of wonderfulness and make your gestures subtle. Think about passing a note to your fellow victim, saying: 'I'd very much like an opportunity to chat at a later date. What say we feign indifference to put them off the scent and then meet for lunch tomorrow?'

3 The party

Pros: Less pressure than a club or bar, because there will be innocent opportunities for a conversation. Social chat is rife at parties and you can easily gain access to someone you lust after without flying under the 'pick-up' banner. This gives you at least one good long conversation in which to impress. Asking someone whether you can get him or her a drink doesn't sound like an overture to sex because you're not paying for the booze. Or you might find an excuse to contact the person after the bash, like mutual membership of the cat breeders' club or the loan of a book.

Younger parties tend to be noisy but old gits tend to allow scope for conversation.

Cons: Walking in alone can be difficult, and so can breaking into conversations.

Body language potential: Body language techniques will increase your effectiveness threefold. Use all the skills explained in the next few chapters to impress.

4 The supermarket

Pros: One of the most popular pick-up places. 'Friendly' atmosphere (if a little sanitised). Gives you a chance to assess his/her taste in groceries and lifestyle first. Casual.

Cons: Muzak is not the most romantic music. The lighting is less than flattering. Genuine shopping – for cat food, pile cream and Tampax – may have to be done somewhere else.

Body language potential: Looking good pushing a trolley takes practice.

Employ the killer walk (read on) and try to look happy and winsome rather than stressed. Use the techniques described earlier for ironing out your face. Imagine you are in an advert for a supermarket, rather than the real thing. If you take kids along, make sure they look terminally cute and low-maintenance. Train them to totter along sucking their thumbs, or ride in the basket of the trolley quietly and cheerfully. Tantrums are not a good selling point. Cute little hats worn at a jaunty angle are. If you can train your toddler to drop its favourite cuddly toy right at the feet of the desirable partner-to-be at a point when you appear not to be looking, then even better.

5 The workplace

Pros: Probably *the* most popular pick-up venue, currently. We work long hours and the workplace is a convenient meeting place. (See the chapter on workplace romance.)

You get to test-drive a potential partner first, seeing him/her in a variety of situations.

You can expand your own potential, too. Long-term relationships of the work-colleague kind mean a broader base to attract from. Workplace romances are notorious for fitting square pegs into round holes. Age and physical attraction barriers tend to fade with time and proximity.

Cons: You may jeopardise your career if the romance turns sour. Stress at work may be multiplied if a relationship becomes hotter, or cools down.

Body language potential: Massive. You can attract and seduce on a long-term basis. If you work on your signals you stand a much better chance of being successful.

6 Hot-desk dating agencies

Pros: You get to meet a large number of potential partners in a very short space of time. Usually the time limit is ten minutes per person. Newer agencies now claim to introduce you to as many as 40 people in one night. When you have chatted for as little as four minutes you put a mark on a card to say whether you would like to meet that person again. If you do, then they put you in touch. It's a very businesslike transaction. No time wasted messing with someone unsuitable. The sheer speed and number of chat-ups involved can make for a degree of fun. The pressure of trying to impress someone in such a very short time span can be alleviated by the very relentlessness of the process.

Cons: How much can you tell about someone in ten minutes? According to the agencies and attendees, quite a lot, actually. The people who pay for this stuff claim attraction is instant and so is dislike. Why waste time wining and dining someone you patently have nothing in common with? And how does the idea of 'never judge by first impressions' apply when many dating agency clients or blind dates scuttle off at the first glimpse of their would-be partner standing under the clock at Paddington station?

Evidentially many of the clients of fast-track agencies are young and good looking. If they are, then they may just be looking for a particular *type* of partner, e.g. blonde, brunette, someone who lives near by, someone who scuba-dives, etc.

There's no scope for revealing hidden strengths – it's all very first-impression based. The thought of multiple rejections could be too much for some people.

Body language potential: The fact that this is all first-impression based gives a lot of scope for chance enhancement. Use the tips in this book on how *not* to display all the old hurts on your face and in your posture. Use open gestures and work on a friendly, confident smile until your face aches. Only use it when it looks right in the mirror. Avoid adopting an assertive, businesslike attitude or you could end up making the process feel like a job interview. The trick is to 'touch' this person – in other words to create a rapport – as quickly as possible.

Look at their body language and posture and leap straight in with a bit of mirroring. Gain empathy by thinking about how they must be feeling and mentioning it. Be funny straight away – witty, not comical. Look congruent by making sure your words, tone and gestures all say the same thing.

7 School or college

Pros: Again, a long, leisurely chance to weigh up your potential partner's attributes. Also a location where you can be spoilt for choice.

Cons: Very public, often with the threat of peer pressure. Difficult to get off with someone you are really attracted to if they lack 'social attraction' attributes. Easier to date someone your entire group will approve of.

Body language potential: Confidence can be the winning card in attraction among this age group. Who dares wins is an important mantra. Using body language to portray confidence is vital. Walk well and think charisma. Imagine at all times that you are taller than your group. Adopt a relaxed facial expression. Imagine you are a supermodel. How would you walk about, gesture and look? Adopt this role-play at all times.

It is vital that you jettison all signals of body hang-ups, like covering yourself with folded arms or speaking with your hand over your mouth. Look proud of every inch of you. Get rid of any jerky movements and loud behaviour. Think cool and confident, even if you're not. Self-esteem is contagious. If you appear to be happy with yourself and your looks, you give people permission to like you and the way you look, too.

8 Singles clubs

Pros: Can be good fun socially as well as for dating.

Cons: Tricky transactions. You are there because you are partnerless and open to offers, so it can be difficult coming up with a way to turn any unwelcome offers down tactfully.

You'll need the initial courage if you go alone, which has got to be the best way if you're looking for a partner. Once there it is often less daunting, though. A bit like a smoking room – instant camaraderie because you're all single. (Although rumour has it that not everyone is totally honest about his/her marital status.)

Body language potential: Enormous. Transactions will be longer, owing to opportunity for social chat and introductions. Plenty of time to let your body language skills enhance your prospects. All tips on flirting and sex signals will be appropriate.

9 The gym

Pros: If you're there to lose weight or tone up, the thought of trying to be attractive at the same time can be hideously depressing. Perhaps women- or men-only gyms might help for the really gruesome stuff and then mixed-sex establishments for the prettier moments or for after the figure starts to become svelte.

However, seeing someone getting moist as they grunt and groan over a few bar-bells will probably give a good enough idea of how their face and body will look when they orgasm.

If you're happy about your appearance sweated up sans slap and in a thong-style leotard, then this could be the ideal place for you to strut your stuff.

Gym camaraderie seems to involve lots of chatting.

Showers seem to be popular single-sex meeting areas.

Many gyms now include posh bar or café areas for socialising après-sweat.

Your skin glows after exercise.

Cons: Exercise doesn't make us all look like Jane Fonda. It's a survival-of-the-fittest-style operation.

Lighting can be dire.

Some of the *real* gyms can get smelly and unsexy.

It can be expensive.

Body language potential: Difficult (and possibly dangerous) to modify your body language during work-outs, although the pool area is the place to get some real bodytalk flirting done.

10 Weddings and funerals

Pros: OK, difficult to engineer, I know, but these provide you with an opportunity to dress up and present yourself in a unique setting. Many of the other guests will be instant deletions as a potential partner, on account of age or the fact that they are blood relations. Most events last several hours, which can lead to opportunities to get together to avoid mutual boredom. Both events form a reminder of our mortality, which is a sexual turn-on. Both also provide an opportunity to display yourself in many different roles, from friend to caring family member to nurturer (playing with any small child-relative that happens to be handy).

Cons: Chat-ups at a funeral can look tacky, especially if you are hitting on the bereaved partner. Also avoid the dance floor at weddings if you have had a few drinks.

Body language potential: Both provide good opportunities to instigate conversations, as your potential audience tends to be trapped in the venue for several hours, which gives you plenty of time to overcome the deletion syndrome. There'll also be a lot of opportunity to show yourself off in different roles, such as 'caring', 'supportive', 'family member', 'fun-lover' (not for funerals), and so on.

Popular, less location-specific methods of meeting include:

The blind date

Pros: Someone who knows you will possibly have set this up, so logically this should mean the other person is some sort of match. However …

If neither of you does a runner at the sight of the other then the chances are you'll have a minimum of two hours to impress him/her with your wit and charisma.

If the date has been set up as a foursome you have other people to talk to and display your personality with.

Cons: The foursome situation is a notorious set-up, with one of the other pair happy to supply Attila the Hun for a date if it means he/she gets to round up numbers.

The fact that you are on 'a date' puts hideous pressure on you to perform.

Body language potential: Lots of potential for making yourself a better match and making yourself more attractive to the other victim, if that's what you want. Employ flirt and listening skills, although start with great subtlety until alcohol loosens your potential partner's inhibitions.

Always stay one drink behind. It's easy to misread someone when you start to get merry, and then you can be deemed to have gone over the top. If you do act like a prat, apologise and say it was because you were nervous and shy. It usually works.

Internet dating

A lot like the traditional blind date, when all is said and done. The fact that you have chatted first on a website will count for nought when you finally get to meet. Soulmates? I don't think so. Physical attraction – or the lack of it – still tends to win or lose the day. Internet dating will make that special moment when you meet in the flesh for the first time even more gruesome. Take everything you have learned about the other person with a pinch of salt until you see them.

There are two rules to remember. First, ensure your safety by meeting during the day, in public. Second, the photo they e-mailed will look nothing like them. If it is blurred that is deliberate and if it is clear then it is of someone else. Try to pitch up looking as much like *your* photo as possible. Otherwise the first thing you will both think when you meet is: 'Liar.'

CHAPTER SEVEN

How to Flirt

It's gird-your-loins time. You've been boosting your inner confidence to the point where you are bursting with the stuff; you've studied ways of making initial contact, and you've matched venue to personal strengths; so now it's time to move on to the next step.

Your next decision will be whether to go out hunting for a mate alone or with friends. Historically the 'pack' method of prowling is more natural, especially when you are younger. Older people, however, increasingly find themselves socialising alone.

Hunting in Packs

The courting ritual for young people has been around for ever. Traditionally young males and young females will work in separate groups. Often they will eye one another up from a distance, while remaining within hearing. Often the first few advances will be anonymous and cheeky, like whistles, cat calls and other signals. These can come from either sex, although they usually come from the men. The women will then look either embarrassed or annoyed. These rituals can go on for a long time. The big challenge is for one of the pack to break away and go and join the other group. When they do, they risk the humiliation of a turn-down in front of their own pack, which is why there will have been a ritual of body language signalling to potential partners prior to this big step.

Most of the exchange will have been through eye contact. The formula is roughly as follows:

1 Getting his/her attention

Young pack members showing off will usually have done this. Loud laughter and mane-tossing is popular with the females, and in some cases bottom displays. For the men it might mean shouting, jostling one another in a playful manner or performing acts in which there is an element of danger.

2 Catching his/her eye

The eye contact stage is meaningful. The eyes meet for approximately one second, which is about half a second longer than a non-sexual glance. One person will then look away in mock embarrassment. Then they will look back, at which point the other person must still be looking. This eye-catching can go on for a whole evening if both parties have the patience. If not, one of the couple, usually the woman, will smile slightly, which gives the man the OK to walk over and start chatting.

3 The meeting

One of the pack walks across to the other and the couple talk. During this stage there will be several preening or grooming gestures, like hair-touching, and some quite dramatic signs of approval, like face-watching and over-loud, exaggerated laughter. Alternatively, females may traditionally take on the shy, diffident role, blushing and looking away while the male talks. Watch some historical dramas and see what sort of giggling, simpering, blushing, dimpling and face-fanning used to go on in more innocent times. While you may think times have changed in the simpering department, in many cases they haven't. Most women would like to think they have evolved beyond the glance-and-giggle stage, but we haven't. Put most of us in the path of an unfeasibly attractive male and we're back to the sort of body language behaviour that would not look amiss in a Southern Belle of the Scarlett O'Hara era.

Women who are both feisty and beautiful have been caught out using similar behaviour. Naomi Campbell in interview will often display in the manner of a shy, flirtatious young girl, ducking her chin and peering through her fringe while giggling and covering her mouth in mock horror if anything shocking is said. Cher adopts a similar technique during interviews, and Britney Spears has perfected the wide-eyes-then-look-away demure glance.

4 Reporting back
At this stage, the individual is still a firm member of the same-sex pack and will report back once the chat-up is finished. If it has been successful there might be a few lewd suggestions; if not then the repair work might include allegations about the exact nature of the sexual preferences of the girl/boy who turned them down.

5 Splitting from the pack
At some stage the relationship may begin to get emotional, and not in the way Vinnie Jones meant when he used the word in *Lock, Stock & Two Smoking Barrels*. When this occurs, the pack member will stop reporting back to the group. This will signal their temporary or permanent removal from the pack.

Ganging Up

In modern life there are still undoubted pluses to hunting in a pack like this. Men need to show that they are a) safe, rather than a lone nutter, and b) sociable and capable of comfortable friendships. Women take a different risk if they work alone – that of looking like a hooker. Clubs and bars are therefore not good 'alone' places. Supermarkets, the workplace and sports clubs, however, are.

If you prefer not to socialise alone, pick the number of your friends carefully. One girlfriend with you implies that you might not want to leave her stranded if you pull, although the number could be handy if your meet a couple of men. Two girlfriends should be OK. Being accompanied by a gay male friend is only good if he doesn't look like your straight partner. Even then it's not the perfect way to pull unless you happen to bump into a straight man out for a night on the tiles with his gay male friend. Gay 'walkers' are usually only suitable for women who either already have or don't want partners or who want to go out in safety.

If you roam in a pack of either men or women, make sure the group doesn't look too closed to approach. Too much laughter and noise can imply you'd turn feral or sarcastic if anyone tried to break in.

Once you've decided to hunt by numbers, the next stage is to perfect your methods of, first, creating sexual interest, and then enticing your potential partner to break away from his/her pack or social group

The held gaze will be your initial ploy in nearly any first-meet situations. This signals interest that extends beyond the 'You're not a deletion' cull, in some cases to the extent of love at first sight. It makes the connection that is necessary for all the moves that follow.

When there is a prospect of seeing this person again under similar circumstances, though – for example, if you have joined an activity club or have met in a group of closer friends – the instantly held gaze may need to be toned down, as it might be less appropriate. In a way it is a distance signal, drawing you out of the pack. If the meeting has been pre-arranged, as in the dinner-party 'making up numbers' situation, the instant gaze signals may need to be omitted completely until much later in the evening. The first-glance routine is difficult to pull off when you know people around you are waiting to see your reaction to the other person. It is also inappropriate at an arranged blind date, or a meeting arranged by an agency. It is a signal of approval. When you know you will be spending time with this person whether you like them or not, the signal will often need to be postponed.

When the relationship is already fixed, as in a workplace situation, where you know you will be seeing the person concerned on a daily basis, the first-glance scenario is very rare, normally happening only on TV or in films. Acting instantly smitten can be dangerous in a workplace situation. The relationship needs to be professional. You may not want to get involved. You may also not want to look like the office Lothario. So save the 'connect' signal for a moment when you are certain it will be deemed appropriate.

Long-distance Flirting

Once your eyes have met across the crowded room, though, many of the initial signals of sexual attraction, like accelerated heartbeat and pupil dilation, will be invisible to your potential mate. This means you may both have to start to indulge in more overt sexual display behaviour to ensure that your message gets across. Balance is important in first-line flirting. Go too far over the top and you can repel by being too obvious. Remember that these are the signals you will be using to keep attention that has already been stimulated by that first look. Although the ritual of the attraction signals that pass between you at this point will be important, nature has managed to ensure that such signals can also be extremely subtle. If someone appears to be ignoring them there is really very little need to press the point, as it probably means they just don't fancy you.

Tips for Women

Women do this long-distant flirting more than straight men, who find it harder. In my experience gay men excel at it. (Stand back, watch and weep.)

For a woman it is an *active* skill, not a passive one. Most women do it without thinking about it. All the women in a group know the minute one of their members has spotted someone she fancies because of the changes in her behaviour. It is the moment she moves from being in the group to signalling to someone outside it.

Traditionally women are accustomed to the role of being the watched, rather than the watcher, during these early stages of a relationship. We are therefore more used to this long-distance performance. On a good day, with the wind behind us, we can walk, talk and fail to trip over while being ogled and assessed by men. We might not always like it, but it is a skill we have to learn.

We therefore have certain posing rituals. Some are good although many are awful.

Good posing rituals

- Smiling appropriately (lips apart, mouth not too far open, the smile also in the eyes).

- Laughing (not too loud, never slapping another person or yourself as you do so – the laugh must look and sound genuine).

- A change in posture. The Miss World pose is a classic that never fails to impress. Bend your right knee in towards the left and extend the right foot out to the side. Allow the pelvis to drop on the right side and push out and up on the left. Hold your drink with both hands at about waist height. (A less girly pose would involve the weight being evenly balanced on both feet with the feet spread within your shoulder span, one hand holding the glass at waist height and the other lightly touching the chin or mouth – though not covering them in a barrier gesture.) The Miss World pose might feel soppy but it's still a winner every time. It makes your legs look slimmer and longer and your hips look smaller and raunchier. As a feminist misdemeanour it doesn't even rate in terms of crimes against the Liberation of Women Act of 1972, so go for it.

- Listening. Use eye contact on the person you are listening to and look genuinely interested in what they are saying. The man watching will admire your ability to focus without distraction. Men like this in a woman.

- The sexual touch. Subtlety is the keyword here, but feel free to indulge in at least one casual sexual touch at this stage. I'll give you a choice: hair, neck, mouth or wineglass. The hair movement needs to be a small, stroking gesture. The neck gesture involves stretching your chin slightly, baring the throat. The mouth gesture should be a very subtle licking of the lips with the tip of the tongue, or a small touch with the tip of the index finger. With the wineglass, stroke the stem with the tip of your finger or rub lightly around the rim. No more than once. And never perform all of these in an attempt to impress, or you could end up looking like a one-woman porno flick.

- A look of vitality. Appear energetic. Imagine you have just walked out of a gym with your eyes glowing, raring to go. Move around rather than looking static or planted. Energy transmits positive signals around the room. Static looks boring.

Bad posing rituals

- Looking bored or distracted. You may think it will give the bloke the cue to come across and rescue you but it will just make you look judgemental and rude.

- Tapping (the foot, a hand, anything). This will show barely disguised aggression.

- Self-comfort gestures, like hair-twiddling, playing with jewellery, nail- or lip-biting.

- Scratching. Anywhere.

- Hiking underwear about.

- Standing with legs spread wide apart – a sign of aggressive superiority, not sex.

- Standing with legs bent outward at the ankle. Girly and pathetic.

- Sucking or eating any slice of fruit in the drink. Could look erotic in a movie but in real life it just looks greedy-guts.

- Sucking your fingers after eating (for the same reason).

- Pulling your hair over your face. A concealment gesture.

- Stuffing tissues up your sleeve or into a pocket after blowing your nose.

- Trying to look confident and in charge (normally ends up looking a bit 'Princess Anne').

- Fussing over other people. Looks nannying, not nurturing.

- Pointing or wagging a finger.

- Not looking as though you are having a good time.

- Looking as though you are having too good a time.

- Frequent, fast blinking or erratic, jerky gestures (looks neurotic).

- Frowning.

- Staring.

- Doing the long-suffering, mouth-shrug smile.

- Keeping your arms folded across your chest.

- Standing with your hands clasped in a low 'sling' at pelvic level.

- Allowing your shoulders to droop.

- Keeping your shoulders too high (looks stressed).

- Snorting when you laugh.

- Flicking your hair about (makes you look like a deranged pony).

- Touching your nose (looks as though you are lying).

- Grooming any other man, e.g. picking a thread off his jacket or dusting away dandruff (makes you look like a fusspot and/or already spoken for).

- Clapping and rubbing your hands (too *Blue Peter*).

Dancing displays

One form of female display is the dance. Some women are so addicted to this method of body display that they will break out in a little routine at the drop of a hat, whether music is playing or not. The idea is to shimmy about revealing body rhythm and potential sexual choreography. Most dance routines include the arms-in-the-air body stretch, which can reveal the midriff and navel, and lots of bottom-wiggling, which can become very overt. No need for Freudian analysis with most of these gestures, although later in the book you'll find more about body parts and their meanings and signals.

All I can say here is that if you are going to dance with the purpose of body display to the boys, then take a few lessons first. At the very least watch your own performance in a mirror and do some work to hone it. You don't have to look like one of the cast of Riverdance to score, but a little ease and fluidity of movement can help.

Alcohol only *appears* to assist dance movement. All it really does is remove inhibitions to the point where you cease caring what you look like. Which is very bad news if you are trying to pull, unless the object of your desire is legless as well, in which case he may not notice.

If you are all for Isadora Duncan-style freedom of expression, then fine, but don't expect your crazy leaping and arm-flinging to say much that is positive about your sexual prowess in bed.

Tips for Men

For blokes, opportunities for effective long-distance flirting are limited. Your body language role models are limited to possibly two: Leslie Phillips and Groucho Marx. You have probably done a brief impersonation of at least one of these in your time.

Long-distance flirting is an almost passive skill for men, which means less is more. Most women prefer their men a little laid back. Watch out for too smooth or suave, though. James Bond only works when James Bond is doing it. Even Robbie Williams struggles with it. Steer clear of similar routines.

Good posing rituals

- Standing chatting to other blokes, but in a casual, not too involved manner, not in a pack. Male bonding is all very well, but not if it appears exclusive and predatory.

- Looking about subtly. Too much room-scanning can look as though you are on the prowl, which suggests you'll settle for anything.

- Getting into conversation. Women like a man who can talk.

- Looking interested in the person you are listening to. The skill of great listening can be as rare as hen's teeth. Practise the art with pride.

- A good laugh and smile. Watch Tom Cruise, John Travolta and even Jack Nicholson. They all have smiles that light up the screen. The smiles look natural but electric. Nearly all current male stars that appeal to women have a similar talent. The smiles are so good they are almost used as a weapon. Practise the smile in a mirror. Hone it until it is magical. It is one of the best tools in your toolkit.

- A frown. No, I'm not being contradictory. It is very effective to do the frown and then throw in a dazzling smile now and again. Get the frown right and you will look focused, serious and in charge. Watch David Beckham. He might wear sarongs, thongs and diamonds, but the frown is sexy and manly. Again, please rehearse this look before going public with it.

- Avoid props. Never lean against anything, like a bar, because this looks too low-energy. Stand upright, and focus on the chest area. A well-developed chest is very attractive to women, especially on a lean body. If you keep your shoulders back and pushed down your hands will hang naturally and feel less awkward. Put the weight on one hip to give a lean, casual look.

- Movement. Stand still for too long and you look like a plonker. Be high-energy. Think fit and active. Women fancy sportsmen and athletes because we like their body language. Straighten up and think like you could manage three hours in the gym.

- The good drinker. Enjoy your drink, but don't guzzle. Hold the glass at lower chest height. Don't study the bottom as though looking for the meaning of life. Use your drink as a prop, not as your sole focus of the evening.

- Stand tall. Raise your chin slightly when you spot someone who attracts you. Then drop it back again, slowly.

- Soften the eyes slightly.

- Put your hand in a pocket, but only if you have practised in the appropriate clothing first. Most men have learnt about the hand-from-belt dangle in other body language books. The idea is that the hands create penis-awareness in the woman: 'Hey, look, I have a willy!' Do this subtly or don't do it at all. We know what you're up to.

- Get a bit of pelvic action going. A very slight movement backward and forward can send out the right signals, but only do it once. Any repetitions and we're off down pervert alley.

Bad posing rituals

- Scratching, picking and other negative grooming.

- Bouncing from the balls of the feet onto the toes.

- Hunching over your glass.

- Opening your mouth wide before you swallow your drink.

- Any ploy you read in dodgy old body language books done in an obvious manner, like resting the thumbs in the belt-loops so that the fingers point towards the crotch, etc. I'm sorry, these are way too corny and crass. You might as well unzip your flies and wave the thing around to get attention.

- Propping one foot up on the foot-rail of the bar.

- Spreading the legs too wide.

- Any hair rearranging gesture.

- Any gesture that looks as though you are still doing some sort of work-out, like neck rolls or calf stretches.

- Any crass expression of recognition and attraction, like raising the eyebrows when your eyes meet those of a person you fancy. (You may as well throw in a moustache twirl, for good measure.)

- Any face-stroking that makes it look as though you're checking whether you shaved OK that morning.

- Folding your arms tight under your armpits.

- Trying to shove your hands into the pockets of your jeans.

- Staring.

- A grin that could be called a leer.

- Nudging your mate in the ribs to point out the person you fancy to them. Then both laughing.

- Show-off routines, like throwing peanuts into the air and catching them in your mouth.

- Rubbing your thighs.

Abandoning the Past

One of the most unattractive things you can wear when you meet someone new is the past. Dragging old baggage into the room with you will decrease your chances of creating fresh relationships that work.

Leave the past at home when you go out. Imagine each day is a new one, and that you travel without clutter. The only experiences you will be packing for the journey are positive ones.

When you meet someone new you will increase your attraction for him or her if you come clad in self-like and the expectation of a positive experience.

Think: Which fruit would I buy in the supermarket, those that are fresh looking or the bruised stuff that has been left at the bottom of the box?

How you wear your bruises

- Eye contact is troubled and fleeting. This registers that you expect a negative response from people who look at you.

- Eye contact is too challenging. This suggests you expect conflict.

- Eyes look rounded and miserable, revealing all the trauma of your past.

- Eyes look blank. You appear distant and preoccupied.

- Blink rate is rapid. You look nervous or stressed.

- Brows are knitted into a frown.

- A smile is stifled, by placing a hand to your mouth, by pursing your lips, by pulling your mouth in, by biting your lip, or by doing the upturned smile, where the corners of the mouth are actually pulled down. This implies you haven't had much reason to laugh in your life.

- Doing the mouth shrug, a downturned smile that implies you are being brave and battling on.

- Rubbing a hand across your face when you speak, which makes you look ill, tired or in pain.

- Sighing when you speak (ditto).

- Protecting your body or your face with your hands, using them as barriers. This shows discomfort, which implies you are unhappy with the way you look.

- Making continual readjustments to hair or clothing. A couple of self-groom gestures can register attraction, but more will display a lack of confidence in your appearance, which will imply you have taken criticism in the past.

- Settling body weight into the pelvic area. Sounds sexy but it looks as though you are trying to make yourself disappear. A low-energy posture.

- Flapping the hands a lot as you talk, which gives the impression you believe you are talking nonsense.

- Laughing at the end of every statement, which creates the same effect.

- Smiling too much, often accompanied by nodding too much. This makes you look too compliant, which suggests you are a doormat.

- Rocking, either on your feet or sitting down. A self-comfort gesture that can appear deeply traumatised.

- Hugging your glass tight to your chest or curling your body around a bag or folded arms. This hedgehog reaction is the complete protector. You look as though you feel surrounded by criticism and negativity.

- Wearing loud colours or a flashy garment. This might make you feel confident and positive but it can often come across as a detractor, deployed to draw attention away from the real you.

- Making too many gestures that show a desire for the approval or support of others. (Not the object of your desire, but other people you happen to be in conversation with when he/she first sees you.) These include watching their faces with wide eyes and quick glances as you speak; 'over-mirroring' – excessive copying of others' expressions and gestures; tapping arms to maintain attention as your speak; bending to look up into others' faces; and backing down and falling silent the minute someone interrupts.

Any and all of these gestures will imply you don't like yourself very much. And if *you* don't like yourself, how can you expect anyone else to?

Self-involvement

A bruised look can be deadly in the attraction process, but so can arrogance. Just when you thought it was safe to come out of the shy closet and try something more confident, a few words of warning about overconfidence. If you appear much more confident than the person you like you might be seen as intimidating. Too many self-like gestures could look like vanity. Avoid the following:

- Too much self-touching that looks vain, such as constant hair-stroking, chest-caressing, cleavage- or shoulder-touching, lip-licking, or sticking fingers into your mouth.

- Tilting your head back too far. Looking down your nose appears arrogant.

- The smug, self-satisfied smile.

- Exaggerated hand gestures.

- Gulping in a large mouthful of air with your mouth open before speaking.

- Holding your cigarette at face height in between puffs.

- Interrupting other speakers.

- Constantly using the 'I' word.

- Speaking while you are eating.

- Taking the mickey out of a mate.

• Whispering.

• Standing with your hands in your pockets and your pelvis pushed forward (men only).

Creating a Unique Response

So now you've shown your potential mate how you interact socially with other people and you've started to show them how you will interact with them. Any moment now it will be time to reveal a facet of your personality *to them alone*. This will be the first piece of behaviour that will demonstrate that your attraction is something special, and that you are singling them out from the rest of the pack. You have already done this to some extent with your eye contact; now's the time to do it verbally or physically. At this point it will be little more than a shy or nervous smile that will contrast with your overall air of confidence. You will work on this later, once the relationship starts to kick off. It will begin to develop trust as you disclose a side of yourself that you have not disclosed to the rest of the social pack.

It is this alteration in response which is vital to making the first connections in a relationship.

CHAPTER EIGHT

Getting into Position

Once you have made some sort of contact with the other person you are going to have to move on quite quickly, while the magic is still working. Easy. If you are at a party or a bar, turn your body in his/her direction. Never stand side-on or with your back to them – the first will make a further glance difficult to choreograph and the second will look like a refusal. Position yourself so as to achieve physical empathy with the other person. (You can do empathy at any distance.) Mirror their pose slightly. Like-bodied looks like-minded – we tend to warm to people sending out similar body signals. By facing your target and mimicking their general style you will already have started to form a duo.

The Approach

You will want this to appear casual to avoid embarrassment. Breaking off from your group and approaching someone from another group is a big step. This is why in some cases the watching and exchanging glances stage can go on all evening and still come to nothing because one of you bottles it.

You will probably feel more comfortable if you can break away from your group for another reason, to provide a sort of 'halfway house' – for example, going to refill your drink. If you do this you should understand that the other person will be watching to see what you do next. If you pause and look around the room as though deciding who to talk to you will probably catch their eye. If you smile and the smile is returned you can now walk over and introduce yourself.

All this is easy if you are either alone or in a loosely structured group. In a party pack, though – a tightly formed group of friends – you'll find the casual intro a lot more difficult. Your group will realise you have gone and what you are up to. Or you will have to announce to them that you are about to go off on the pull. Their inquisitive body language will send signals to the person you want to approach, and the pressure to turn you down out of embarrassment will be strong.

This is one reason why venues like supermarkets and even the workplace are growing in popularity as the place to meet. They create scenarios that make the necessity of finding a halfway house redundant. You get it on a plate, as long as you engineer arrival in the same checkout queue, or even staring at the same tin of beans on the shelf, at the same time. In the workplace long-term proximity creates a legion of excuses to chat.

The blind date, or meeting arranged by a dating agency, will mean you get to do the approach before you register visual interest. By the time you meet you have already announced that you are on the hunt for a partner. This tends to jumble the messaging system, which is built to cope with the 'Well, hello!' style of ritual. With the blind date you need to start with polite social signals and register your attraction (if there is one) later in the meeting. This will come during the 'moment', the 'connect' signal that both of you should understand. Often this is the point where you show empathy by laughing together. As you laugh your eyes should meet for the magic look that registers interest.

If it feels by now that your eyes have been doing all the work and are about to fall out of their sockets with fatigue, don't worry. The next big gun in your arsenal of sexual weaponry is about to be produced. Eye contact is easy. Your next ace is a more difficult skill to manage, but I guarantee the sweat and effort will be repaid in results. You're about to invest some time learning:

The Drop Dead Walk

Creating a first impression at most social occasions might include walking across a room. For women, this is a perfect opportunity to shine. A good walk can be literally breathtaking, no matter how low you rate in terms of social attraction. It is a true taster of your sexual behaviour and prowess. Get it right and you get a chance to display your techniques of timing and choreography. For men it means a chance to become terminally attractive, a real sexual animal, rather than just another bloke.

Catwalk models perfect the ultimate sensual walk, which can floor a man at 60 paces. But any woman can turn on a good walk, one of the most effective weapons in her armoury, whatever her size or shape. You don't have to be a willowy, size eight six-footer (although I must say it helps).

Most people walk very badly, a bit like Forrest Gump. From the moment we start to totter (the kiddie stuff, not the drunken stuff) we are on our own, completely devoid of coaching. Most women make several basic mistakes:

- Leading with the head, the easiest part of the body to propel, which means you keep your head down and look at the floor.

- Allowing the shoulders to slump. This gives a low-energy look. You seem to lack that vital spark.

- Letting the arms hang forward.

- Arching the back and sticking the bottom out.

- Bending the legs from the hip joint.

- Banging the heel down first.

- Not bending the feet.

- Propelling themselves by swinging the arms.

Remembering that a good walk is your most precious asset, keep in mind Marilyn Monroe's assertion that people often ignored her in the street until she put on 'the walk'. You are going to have that same power, which will make all the time devoted to perfecting it worth the work. Follow these basic steps:

- All the effort of your DD Walk should be concentrated in your feet. Therefore you need shoes that will bend as you move. You will be peeling your feet off the floor and propelling yourself from the ball of the foot and the toes. This will be harder in very thick-soled shoes. Wear something flexible.

- Most women can't cope with a very high heel. To compensate for their effect they often stick their bottoms out, which makes them walk like chickens. Stilettos may be in fashion, but stick to something a little lower if you can't cope.

- Stand in front of a full-length mirror.

- Pull your spine up as though you are trying to touch the ceiling with the top of your head.

- Breathe in and then let the breath out again – your body should now feel tall but relaxed.

- Circle your shoulders until they are held back, but dropped down.

- Shake your hands a little to help the muscles relax.

- Touch the sides of your legs with your fingertips. When you begin to walk, allow your arms to sway a little, but as a natural result of your body movement.

- Tuck your bottom in and under and push the lower pelvis forward. You can exaggerate this technique while you are learning, but tone it down when you do the DD Walk for real. Think catwalk model. You are going to learn to lead from the lower hip. When you do this you will realise why a catwalk is called a *cat*walk. You feel like a panther when you get this walk right. Unfortunately you look like a hippo with a hernia if you get it wrong. It's not as hard as it sounds, though.

- Now, as part of the catwalk-clone look, put your right foot out and touch the floor with the big toe. As you push the leg out, try to twist the right side of the pelvis forward too, so that you turn from the waist, rather than bending from the hip joint.

- Place the ball of the foot down first and then the heel. If you watch current catwalk models you'll probably see them putting the heel down first, but this is part of the recent naturalist look. The models of a previous generation would have done the glide, and this is the technique you're going to study first.

- Focus on moving the pelvis in a smooth roll from side to side, along with the relevant leg. Move smoothly and think like a cat. Allow your pelvis to lead. Think sexy. If you go wrong just stop and start again.

- Take a slightly smaller stride than normal. The point of this walk is not when you arrive but what you do en route.

When you have perfected this smooth, sinewy, cat-like walk, start toning it down for everyday use. You don't need to walk down the street like this, but you will improve your normal walk as you practise the technique. Save the DD Walk for key moments – such as walking into or across the room at a party. You can turn a trip to the loo into a moving advertisement for your sensuality (the walk *to* the loo, not what you do when you get there, obviously).

For men

- Think of the areas of the body that you want to display and feature as you walk. Focus on those a potential mate is likely to be most attracted to: face, chest and groin.

- Think how you can display these while you walk (although 'subtlety' could be a word to bear in mind here!).

- Visualise a walk that is fluid, easy looking and relaxed.

- Avoid anything that looks fussy or appears to exert too much effort.

- Pull yourself up to your full height by stretching your spine.

- Breathe in and then out again slowly to release inner, pent-up tension and give the posture a relaxed, while still upright, look.

- Focus your energy into your shoulders. Rotate them in a circle, while keeping your arms down by your sides. Stop when they are held back and down.

- Don't adopt a pose that looks too military.

- Pull in your stomach and tuck your bottom in slightly.

- Brush your fingertips lightly against the sides of your legs.

- Walk in front of a mirror and try to judge what seems the correct stride for your leg length. Shorter men have a tendency to over-stretch in the stride, which looks awkward.

- Allow the arms to swing naturally with your body motion as you walk.

- Allow your fingers to relax. Don't form them into fists or you'll look like Popeye after he's been eating spinach. The hands should be slightly cupped with the fingers curved.

- Don't lean forward. Keep the body upright.

- Put the heel of the foot down first, then peel onto the ball of the foot, so that the toes propel you into the next step.

- Move your hips slightly from the waist as you walk. This gives the walk a coordinated movement.

- Imagine you are James Dean or Clint Eastwood. Laid back but tough.

Style Variations

There are some celebrities who have adopted their own signature walks or poses. If you think they look cool you might want to copy them. Do so at your peril, though, as most of them look a little affected.

The Grant Mitchell

This look is beloved of bouncers and work-out fanatics across the globe. It is characterised by the fact that the arms and chest are developed to the point where the bicep muscles prevent the rest of the arm having contact with the torso, leading to a teapot-with-two-handles effect. If you want to look menacing, this is the one for you.

If you are the runt of the litter, this pose could bulk out your top half a little.

The Victoria Beckham/Liz Hurley

This involves standing well, with a good straight spine and shoulders, but then holding the arms back and tucking the elbows into the waist so that the arms below the elbow stick out at the sides. It has the effect of turning the bosom into a formal presentation. It also makes the woman look rather fey and fragile, despite the well-proportioned knockers out front.

Try it first only in the privacy of your own home.

The Cilla Black/Davina McCall

This 'ladette' look involves keeping the arms glued to the torso from shoulder to elbow in a form of self-comforting body hug. With the Cilla, the arm from elbow to wrist is used to gesture, while in the Davina the hands are joined tightly at waist level in a form of mock apology for all the often quite daring fun her shows are known for.

The Bush/Blair

These two present the modern face of political posture. Success in the noughties is equated with fitness. Both men stand well, with a strong shoulder focus that is almost reminiscent of Superman.

The pin-up pout

Glamour models and their movie counterparts have a pose that sets off their particular body shape (large breasts, short bodies) to best advantage. Kylie Minogue uses this posture to great effect. The skill is in the very acute arch of the spine. The bottom must be pushed right out, the body drawn in again at the waist, then the shoulder blades arched back out. It is as though you are trying to form a letter C with your spine, and has the advantage of making both your breasts and your buttocks a feature. Drop your chin and pout like a small child who wants sweets and you more or less have it. (This pose is harder to do than it looks, and some training in dance is helpful if you don't want to end up in the osteopathy department of the local hospital.)

So now you've mastered the art of attracting and holding attention through techniques such as your newly improved posture and drop dead walk. In the short term you've convinced the object of your desire that you have the makings of a sex god/goddess. Now it's time to move on to some more close-up techniques.

CHAPTER NINE

How to Make Yourself Desirable

The Decision to Buy

You are now ready to progress to the next stage of the process, in which you will start to talk and use eye and ear listening skills to monitor this new person and find out whether your first impressions have been accurate or wide of the mark.

If you are a man the die is probably already cast by now: most women know whether or not they will have sex with a man within the first five seconds of meeting him. But don't get too excited by this. We spend a lot longer waiting for you to talk us out of our original decision. Many men who believe they are talking, joking or seducing a woman into bed are doing just the opposite. She originally decided she would and he is now busy boring her out of that first positive appraisal.

For women

For a woman, deciding she *would* or *might* is not the same as wanting to jump into bed straight away. It's just a mental assessment, not statement of intent. 'I would' does not mean the same as 'I will'. There is still a lot of water that needs to pass under the bridge first.

Women may organise men into quite clearly defined categories, labelled 'Would', 'Wouldn't' and 'Might'. The 'Mights' need to show some extra potential if they are to move into the 'Would' pile. This upgrade (or downgrade) can come about with the revelation of a surprise factor. For example, you discover after talking to them that they:

- Are funnier/warmer/more intelligent than you thought.

- Are more interesting than they look.

- Are kinder than you'd imagined.

- Dress better than you thought.

- Could be persuaded to dress better.

- Are rich.

- Have a nice car.

- Are commissioning editor at a TV station.

Yes, I know these last four are hugely superficial, but then not every girl's looking for a winner of the Nobel Peace Prize.

For men
Do men just have one pile labelled 'Would' with 'Depending how drunk I am' scribbled underneath? Of course not. Men have a deletion pile, too, although they tend, as I have said, to look less to a positive future than women do. They like to like what they see and are less prone to being 'surprised' into a re-evaluation by noting that the woman is richer, more powerful or even drives a nicer car than they thought. For a man these qualities are not sexually impressive, and can even be seen as threatening.

Getting Ahead

Making yourself desirable to the person you want as a mate has – as I said in the first chapter – no 'one size fits all' formula. But you can enhance your mating potential by employing a few tricks. The instant attractors mentioned earlier will be used to maximise that first-glance moment which ensures that you connect. Stage two involves conversational techniques and a more complex ritual of body language signalling.

For men
Partly the technique of attraction for men is the strategy of more is less. Imagine the point in a football match when one

team is 1–0 up and there are ten minutes to go. The strikers have all pulled back to join the defenders. All they have to do is keep the score stable.

This is very much the man's role once the first signals of attraction have been exchanged. You don't have to chat the girl up or dazzle her with your wit or ability to entertain. Most women are soon bored by both – we only pretend to find it amusing because to a great extent we have already made our decision about your suitability. The social attraction element has been taken care of: either we think you already look right or we guess you might scrub up well with a little patience and a few lengths of MDF. All we're hoping is that you are interesting enough company with no disgusting habits.

This is where many men let themselves down. They feel they still have to keep trying, even when the main part of the battle's won. They go for the 'chat-up' that only ever draws gasps of admiration from their mates. When men say a bloke is good at chatting girls up, women immediately know that he is a grade-A embarrassing bore. The fact that he still manages to pull means that:

- He has all his own teeth and hair (and perhaps a Porsche).

- He takes the plunge and chats to women in the first place.

- He pulls *despite* the chat-up routine, not *because* of it.

When you see a woman giggling at this kind of chat-up you need to understand one thing about body language: people often use these 'approval' signals when they feel awkward. It is a form of politeness. We do it to overcome our embarrassment, not because we are genuinely amused. I have listened to some of the worst jokes in the world and laughed at the punch-line because I was too embarrassed to do anything else. The worse the joke, the more I have laughed. Ditto with the old chat-up routine. The more crass it is, the more you tend to smile. If you want to see whether a woman's smile is genuine or not, look at the eyes.

The same applies to the 'flash and boastful' routine, during which the man does everything but wave his bank balance in the air, and the boyish, playful puppy-dog act, which can be cute enough to make you want to vomit.

Try putting on less of an act. Don't display too much too soon. Women like a bit of a psychological challenge. We prefer to be intrigued rather than swamped.

The first stage

Spatial behaviour is important. When you speak to someone for the first time, make sure you keep to the appropriate area. Height is an issue. The taller you are, the farther away you need to stand. No woman likes to peer up a man's nostrils, and the extra height can make you appear imposing and possibly threatening. This doesn't mean you need to converse from the next room – just adjust the space between you to make it possible for the woman to talk to you without getting neck-ache. At most social functions the normal position for an average/shorter man would be a small pace apart. Any farther and you will appear aloof. Any closer and you will feel threatening and invasive.

At a noisy club, however, spatial behaviour can be more intimate, because you will need to break many of the social rules just to talk to one another. Clubs give you the opportunity to whisper in the woman's ear, which you would normally only do after you have known one another for a while, but if you don't do it in this situation you won't be heard. This leaning closer might also involve a light touch, which would otherwise be inappropriate. (This doesn't mean that you should hit the clubs on the basis that they provide an ideal scenario for the frotteur.) This gives you a chance to fast-track your body language, although the general sound level might mean that any verbal subtlety or intimacy is negligible.

Face the woman, but not completely full-frontal. Blocking out the rest of the room may ensure attention but it also seems predatory. Stand very slightly side-on, with most of your torso and face turned in her direction, to register interest. Never stand looking away, as you will appear either bored or as though you are still intent on scanning the room for other interesting prospects. Keep your feet no more than shoulder width apart and never fold your arms, which can look dominant and critical.

It is vital at this stage that you register undivided attention.

You will be moving the relationship into something more personal and intimate and, by appearing attentive at this point, you have the chance to single the woman out and – in attention rather than physical terms – take her away from the rest of the room. Similarly your goal is to get her full and undivided attention, but without being flash or acting the fool.

Use full eye contact while you are listening, but vary it slightly when you are talking, or you may appear aggressive. You are aiming for long periods of sustained eye contact between the two of you. When the eyes connect – even for a short period – you begin to communicate on a far deeper level. People around you will notice this connection subconsciously and begin to leave you alone.

Choose a moment to try to make the eye contact more meaningful. There's something about sustained eye contact which is magical. It can feel as though the other person is reaching right into your soul. Avoid the blank-eyed stare, though, which looks creepy and aggressive. Put a message into your eyes. Go for broke. Imagine you are trying to say 'You are the most amazing woman I have ever met'. Let that thought come into your eyes. (It's OK, you don't have to commit and say it out loud.)

Use active listening techniques, like nodding and allowing your facial expressions to react to the dialogue. Avoid looking as though you can't wait for your turn to speak. Also avoid letting your eyes drop to the rest of her body at this point. You should have noticed all that before you made your approach. Doing it now will look crass.

Create rapport and empathy. When the woman talks about something that happened to her, try to sum up her feelings correctly, as in: 'That must have been annoying for you', or 'You must have been very upset'. Men rarely use this insight technique but it shows depth of thinking and an interest in the woman's feelings. If you guess the emotion correctly you will probably hit pay dirt. Remember something she said at the start of the conversation and refer back to it. This will show you have been listening. I promise you, she will be impressed.

Once you have tried the meaningful eye contact (only briefly

– a couple of seconds should do the trick, not the complete Mesmer routine), go for the first flirt signal. Look the woman in the eye, then allow your eyes to fall down to her mouth, then raise them to her eyes again. Do this with the hint of a smile that says: 'My God, you're lovely' (not 'You have a chunk of broccoli between your front teeth').

For women

Generally women need to be rather more active at this stage in the transaction. Bette Davis may have been able to recline with a fag and have men grovelling at her feet, but those days are sadly past, if they ever existed in reality.

The days of waiting for the man to make the first move have also gone, although some men – particularly older ones – still prefer to stick with this little ritual. It's the first definition of power in the relationship, although the man usually feels anything but powerful as he makes his approach.

The rules of engagement have changed, but not always as much as we'd like to think. In most of my research with under-twenties I noticed that many still stuck to the boy-makes-the-first-move rituals of their grandparents' generation. In some cases the boys still thought they should be responsible for paying on a date.

If you feel like being fey, then allow the man to make the first approach.

The first stage

Pull yourself up to your full height, even if you are tall. Arch the back slightly, so that your breasts lift and your bottom sticks out. Bend one knee in towards the other leg. (You used these posture techniques to create the initial attraction, so don't blow it now by sagging or stooping.)

Drop your chin slightly as he is talking and look up into his face. Smile as you do so (a pouty, puckered smile – no teeth), or you could look disapproving. Then, at a certain point (preferably when he pays you a compliment or says something funny – if you have to wait too long for either of these key moments, seriously consider bolting for the exit, unless he drives something *wonderful*, like a yacht), arch your neck. This will enable you to bare your throat at him, which can be seen as immensely erotic, and not just by vampires – probably because it provides a kind of Cresta run for the eyes, leading straight down into the cleavage. One tip to maximise the effect of this little manoeuvre: keep your neck bare of chains or other jewellery, as it spoils the clear-run effect. The vulnerability of the neck will signal a blossoming level of trust in the relationship, too. If you have already used this gesture from a distance don't worry too much about trying it close up as well. (In fact, you can also give it a big whirl during sex itself, if you get that far. If the man has been reared on a diet of porn, then he may well expect it as the norm. It's something of a classic pose. Think Rod Stewart or Liam Gallagher singing at the mike.)

Touch your neck lightly with one hand. For any man still stupid enough to be unaffected by the neck-arch gesture, this should be the equivalent of supplying subtitles. Don't allow this gesture to look nervous. It should never be confused with the 'Mavis Riley' neck-flutter that registers dither rather than sensuality.

Hold your drink at a level where the rim of the glass will meet your breasts. Never hold it with both hands as this will give the appearance of someone holding a begging bowl, and therefore look desperate. The way you hold the glass is important, as it may be interpreted as giving hints as to your sexual technique. Keep your grip light, and caress the stem subtly with one finger now and again as he is speaking.

Point at least one of your feet towards the man. This means very little in reality but – for some reason – many men set a lot of store by the gesture. It is one of those body language urban legends that refuses to die. Ditto crossing your leg towards him if you sit down.

The biggest flirt technique for women is probably the most obvious one: whatever you do, look interested in what he has to say. The ability to listen well, or to indulge in what the Americans call 'aerobic listening', is one of the mainstays of charisma and a solid-gold flirt technique. Men love to be the centre of attention. It reaffirms or enhances their role as leader of the pack, or at least gives the suggestion of group dominance. If he comes from a large family, this devoted attention will be what he will have fought for throughout his entire childhood; if he is an only child, it is what he will have grown to expect as his right. Undivided attention is the sucker punch that most men fall for – even shy men, who will still be happy with just one person in attendance.

Listening well, or at least *looking* as though you are listening well, is easy. Use eye contact. Nod as he speaks. This registers empathy and understanding. Pace the nod to suit the subject matter – fastish for football or boastful stories, slower for work-related issues, and slower still for divorce or bad health stories or other emotional issues. Lean forward slightly. Face him full-on.

Most men enjoy two facial expressions in women: 'fun' and 'sympathetic'. These will provide all the hints they need that they have discovered the best buddy/sex siren/mummy substitute they have spent their lives searching for.

Both expressions need to be worked mainly from the eyes. If you place too much emphasis on mouth movement you may end up looking insincere. 'Fun' comes from a slight narrowing of the eyes, although you should keep moving your gaze from his eyes to his mouth, as though amused by what he is saying. Combine this with a suppressed smile – the lips held together and one or both corners of the mouth turned up, much as though you are trying not to smile but are losing the battle.

'Sympathetic' is achieved by adopting a slight frown of concern, creating an expression in the eyes as though you have just heard that his dog has died (which may well be true), leaning forward slightly and nodding slowly. Keep the eye expression soft rather than wide or cold, which will be seen as uncaring.

As men get older their craving for these two emotions in one woman intensifies, which is why you should perfect them if you are choosing an older man. As a general rule of thumb, the older you get the more problems you suffer, so sympathy turns into a desirable quality rather than the affectation of a patronising ratbag. Keep the sympathy for more private moments, though. Many men tell stories of hardship in public to elicit gasps of admiration rather than tears of empathy. (I know this is a book about body language, but one verbal tip I have picked up which needs to be mentioned here is that women should avoid responses like 'You're joking!' or 'I don't believe it!' when being told by men about tragedy or emotional upset. Whereas women use these phrases to register genuine astonishment, men tend to take them literally and assume you think they are lying, or that you find their sadness amusing.) The sympathetic persona is relevant to sexual flirting. Men who are less than confident about their ability to perform in bed may find the sympathetic image sexually attractive, as you will appear less likely to find any form of impotence snigger-worthy.

Mirroring is a good flirt wheeze for women. By slightly copying the man's body language and/or style of behaviour and delivery you will fast-track the bonding process. Anything over-butch is probably best left untouched, but feel free to go for jolly or quiet or close-up or serious. Remember: like-bodied tends to look like-minded.

If all this mirroring and listening is leaving you feeling slightly 'surrendered', don't worry. This stage of the mating process is very much as a job interview is to the job itself – you are employing 'best behaviour' mode to impress your way through to the next stages. If you are both clever you will be aware that the person you are currently interviewing bears very little resemblance to the person you would discover if you dated/had sex with/married them. Your present behaviour is like wearing a smart suit to impress a potential boss. In a way you both know it's not what you wear all the time, but the fact that you are making the effort is – in itself – flattering. Don't think you have no option to change after this initial meeting. Being an industrial-strength ego-masseur at this stage does not mean you can't become more assertive later on.

If you feel that acting strong and playing it cool are more appropriate, though, go for it. Most women can spot the men who will respond well to this type of treatment – the symptoms usually involve being good looking and a bit of a big-head. One rule of life is that people who can have anything they want only want things they can't have. Like being put on the waiting list for a pair of Prada sunglasses, the wait only intensifies the longing. Don't assume that a man is an egotist just because he is good looking, though.

The Bodytalk Striptease

Once you have presented your image to the person you like and have begun to get into conversation, now is the time to start 'stripping'. People like contrast, and it is up to you to deliver it if you want to begin to connect. This 'reveal' technique starts to give the impression that you are allowing the other person to get a glimpse of the real you inside. This is flattering, if it is done well.

For instance, if up to now you have presented yourself as confident, or even loud, brash and funny, a slightly diffident technique now can be hugely appealing. Women like a loud show-off who reveals himself – *to them* – as a bit of a softie. Or an intellectual who can act daft. Or a sex god with shyness problems. Unpeeling the outer layers to reveal the truth within is – for some – an attractive prospect. We like to feel we know the 'real' person, the one who lives behind the bluff. Revealing some of this early on in the potential relationship is a winner. In a way, it fast-tracks the relationship.

Remember: the striptease should never be done verbally, as it will come across as insincere. Telling someone you are really very shy when you have just pole-danced for half an hour will sound crass and manipulative. Implying the same through your body language can look genuine and attractive, though.

This layer-peeling is an important tool in your attraction toolkit. It is not the same as looking false faced, merely a technique for allowing a quick peek at your hidden depths. This is especially important if you present yourself as a bit of a joker or a bit flash. Your skill for entertainment is probably a positive one, but it can only be enhanced if you show a flash of intellect or an ability to be sensitive at the same time. It is also effective if you appear to reveal this side of your character almost exclusively to the person you are attracted to. Overconfidence can be offset by a touch of insecurity, determined jollity by irony or a more soulful side, and sexiness by innocence. Do this successfully and you could well transform yourself into a human magnet.

The Presenting Persona

What type of character do you tend to present when you are out socially? Are you loud or quiet, shy or extrovert? Will you tell jokes and be physically active, or still and sophisticated? Is your charm puppy-like or suave? Do you present as raunchy or regal?

Understanding your overall image is a vital first step towards unpeeling. If you are unsure, ask friends who tend to be honest. *Always* ask partners how they felt you presented at your first meeting. If the relationship fails then at least you can emerge with this piece of valuable information to take into your next mating opportunity. Once you are aware of your presenting style you can work out how to slip in those little hints of contrast.

If you have trouble visualising the effect, think of leading characters in the soaps. What the viewing public tends to warm to in them is a contrast in their characters – the greater the contrast between those two personas, the more we tend to like them. Most soaps have a brassy female lead, like Bet Lynch or Kat Slater. Their presenting style is the sort that would make most people run a mile if they saw them in a pub. They are loud and often aggressive. But what works on us is the complete contrast beneath the brassy exterior. We know all about their tragedies and their insecurities. The same applies to an aggressive male character. Grant Mitchell was bearable and even lovable because we knew he'd had his heart broken.

I'm not suggesting that you present like any of these characters, but the idea is one that can be copied, albeit in a toned-down way.

You need only drop one small hint of your hidden depths during this first meeting. Any more and the depths will no longer be hidden. They will become part of your presenting persona, and then you will be looking for something else to unpeel. Next thing you'll be talking about your train set in the attic and how your mummy still makes you a hot-water bottle each night. This type of unpeeling is unlikely to be considered remotely attractive.

Added Value

I referred to the different levels of attraction at the beginning of the book – how we look for someone with social appeal, but also someone who connects with past comforts. This technique of unpeeling can also help you hedge your bets with someone by offering a glimpse of someone else. If the current persona fails to connect, then the alternative version may well do the trick.

I once witnessed a devastating case of this involving a young waitress in a restaurant. She was trendy and casual, and the group of middle-aged men she was serving obviously expected her to be on a different level to them in just about every way. Then she dealt the killer blow. Something funny happened as she was taking the order and she said, 'Oh, that was very Monty Python, wasn't it?' Suddenly all the men looked up at her, intrigued. She'd made an instant connection with their past. Suddenly she became of interest to them. Until then, they had obviously dismissed her as being someone to whom only their teenage sons could relate. But now contact had been made. Suddenly they were with a gorgeous and interesting young woman, and they kept her endlessly amused with their rendition of the Pythons' dead parrot sketch. Bliss.

I had a similar experience when meeting a famous intellectual who can come across as daunting. I was babbling nervously when he suddenly said something that included a very naughty swear word. He looked surprised at himself and we both laughed like kids. I had been impressed by his great intellect but I knew that there was no connection between us as I prefer to communicate and work in a more down-to-earth manner. The touch of childlike naughtiness did make the connection, though.

Faking It

It's important when using the unpeeling technique that you never stray into the dangerous territory of looking like a phoney. Unpeeling involves presenting your genuine exterior persona and revealing some of the interior stuff at the same time – like wearing a suit but giving someone a glimpse of your underwear. Faking it is different. The 'bold exterior, soft centre' approach *is* attractive. What is less appealing is to try to give the impression of being a happy party animal if inside you are really a sad, whingeing, censorious bore.

Women are less traumatised by some forms of insincerity than men. We are (a sweeping generalisation coming up here, but a commonly held one, too) more people-perceptive than men. We usually find it easier to spot the phoney. But spotting them does not always imply spurning them. That little psychologist who lives inside all of us will often tell a woman that what seems a very obvious incongruity is in reality a sign of vulnerability – that the lie might even be a cover-up for something nicer. We will often see it as a form of childish concealment, clumsily intended to impress, and sometimes this can be seen as flattering.

Where women will not tolerate falseness is within their own sex. Female friends find honesty the most bonding quality. We share more, verbally and emotionally, than men. We expect high standards of openness – except when we ask one another two questions: 'Does my outfit look OK?' and 'What do you think of my new man?' For everything else honesty is non-negotiable, because we can usually spot the lie.

Owing, perhaps, to an inner streak of pessimism, men will tend to view falseness in women as hiding something less nice. They can be more trusting and less able to spot the phoney but, when they do, they will be less likely to view the falseness as a childish weakness – perhaps because it has fooled them in the first place. For women there is security in being able to see behind the lie. For men the fact that the lie caught them out can be devastating. Where women see the small boy hiding behind the teller of tall tales, a man will see Cruella de Ville lurking behind the adorable little girl.

Anti-flirting

When you have made full use of your flirting techniques – giving your potential mate your undivided attention and mirroring their movements – it's time to use a blatant trick.

Once they are happily basking in the glow of your attention, turn it off like a tap for a while. It's a cute but effective little shock tactic, like sitting someone in front of a warm fire until they get cosy and then moving the fire away and exposing them to a cold draught. What happens? They want the fire back. Be subtle but firm. Now that they've seen what they can have, let them see how it feels without it. Withdraw and look away for a while. Hopefully they will appreciate the contrast and try to rekindle the warm fire. Then you turn it on again. It shows them that they have to work for your attention and that you're not a complete pushover.

One factor that might hamper both your self-confidence and your pulling ability at this stage is a tendency to focus to such an extent on your own bodytalk techniques that you are unable to interpret the effect they are having on your potential partner. Do they like you? Do they fancy you? Do they just wish you would go away?

Negative inner dialogues can be destructive, so it's important to spend as much time reading the incoming body language mail as you do on tailoring you own outgoing messages. The next chapter will explain how to read your potential mate's signals from the earliest stages of meeting to the time when things start to get more intimate.

CHAPTER TEN

Do They Like Me? – Reading a Potential Partner's Signals

So how can you tell if someone fancies you? Again, the signals will be complex, but searching for and then reading them will always give you clues, if not solid fact.

In a perfect situation the easiest way for someone to let you know they like you is for them to tell you. Except we rarely have the confidence to do this, because we fear rejection and being made to look a turnip. Teenagers have come up with the perfect solution: they get a mate to tell the object of their desire that they rate them. If the answer is a turn-down they can always say their friend was lying. Easy.

The rest of us have to settle for body language hints, though. These – as I have said – can be misleading, especially in a work situation where staff may send out flirt signals on an almost constant basis, but without true sexual intention. Some social groups will flirt outrageously although everyone has a partner; the unspoken rule is that no one takes things any farther.

To live in society we are forced to balance our sexual signals carefully. If we over-display we are seen as behaving inappropriately and lacking in self-control. If we under-display we are seen as cold, inexpressive and distant. Appropriate behaviour depends on culture and group size, so when you read another person's signals keep both these aspects in mind before relating them to your own perception of what is 'the norm'.

Large cities, for instance, often develop a culture of 'distant' body signals to create safety and isolation. At the epicentre, though, may be a very strong and sexually liberated set of social signals that can shock people from more rural areas, who may have developed a friendlier initial approach but a more formal social sense.

When you look for signals of attraction from a potential mate, please keep all the circumstances in mind. Evaluate every reason as to why this person may be displaying in this way, and make sure a refusal won't offend if you discover you have read these signals wrongly.

Animal Signals

There are certain instinctive signals we send when we are attracted to someone which we may be unaware of ourselves.

Grooming. When we see someone we fancy we often begin a ritual of self-grooming. This may be something as simple as smoothing the hair or straightening the clothes. Women also go in for mate-grooming gestures in order to signal male ownership to other women. Remember how your mother used to embarrass you hideously by making you spit on a hankie to wash your face in the street? Well, unfortunately gestures like these are programmed into every woman's DNA. When a woman straightens your tie or dusts lint or a hair off your jacket, never underestimate the gesture. It is possessive and territorial. She is marking her territory and warning other women off. Think yourself lucky she's not making you spit on a hankie.

Pelvic adjustment. For men the crotch will move farther forward in terms of the overall posture. For women the back will arch and the buttocks move back slightly. (Although close monitoring of the movement of either could land you in trouble in the early stages.)

Waist-trimming. In both sexes there will be an attempt to present the torso in an attractive way. This means the person will stand taller and pull the stomach and waist in.

Flush or blush. The body starts to heat up a few degrees. (Nervousness can also create this effect, though.)

Huskiness. The voice deepens slightly during sexual arousal.

Pupil dilation. This involuntary response is a good indication of intent, although hard to spot from a reasonable distance.

Eye contact. It's hard not to stare when you like someone.

Expect the magic first glance, followed by periods of prolonged 'watching'.

Torso-turning. Men, in particular, tend to point the most prominent part of the body towards the most important person in the room. If his chest faces you, even if his eyes are turned away, this means he is interested.

Muscle-flexing. Often a sign of attraction in men, meaning you've just brought out their protective, manly side. If this posturing ends up as knuckle-cracking, though, you have my sympathy.

Isolation attempts. When someone likes you they will try to separate you, first from your group and then from the rest of the room. Watch to see whether the other person stands directly in front of you when they talk to you, or tries to turn you to face him/her more full-on. Striking full-frontal poses with no barriers between you is often a sign that someone is interested.

Chest-puffing. Both men and women will tend to stick their chest out more. In men this is to signal strength and superiority, and in women it presents the breasts for approval. Breasts are a strong sex signal because they mimic the shape of the buttocks.

Chest-banging displays. Not literally, of course, but the male will often feel the need to show off in some way to the female. This 'chest-banging' gesture can be obvious – boisterous, playful behaviour; muscle-flexing; sporting displays; fast-driving displays; flipping beer mats; opening bottles or ripping packets of crisps open with the teeth; flattening drink cans in one hand; even leapfrogging posts or damaging property – or more subtle – flashing an expensive watch or credit card; displaying knowledge or status symbols, like job titles or car keys; displaying designer labels on clothing; displaying mobile phone qualities, such as ring tone or Internet connection.

These displays are often boring to women, but can be a necessary part of the mating process for men. In younger or emotionally retarded men the chest-banging will continue and the woman will often be invited to the man's place just to watch his prowess at computer games.

Phallic Displays

Lord knows these can often be unintentional, but take note of them anyway. If nothing else they should provide you with a good laugh.

Crotch, bottom, breast displays. These can be performed with a degree of subtlety. A man may push his suit jacket to one side to reveal the crotch area, or find an excuse to lean against something and place one hand in his trouser pocket, drawing attention to his crotch. (Overt and prolonged fiddling with crotch or bottom will mean something a whole lot less pleasant.) A woman may put one hand on her hip, to accentuate the pelvis and buttocks.

Tie-stroking. Could the thing look any more like an arrow pointing towards the penis?

Leg-swinging. A seated woman with her legs crossed may begin to swing the top leg. (If the leg-swing becomes too rapid it could be a sign of boredom or impatience, though.) If she clasps the knee and leans forward a little she is becoming flirtatious and playful. Alternatively, a woman may stroke or smooth the leg with one hand, or allow one shoe to drop off the heel of the foot and dangle.

Mouth-touching. A woman may touch her mouth with the tip of the index finger or lick her lips. Wiping the corner of the mouth with one finger, as though rubbing away a crumb, is different, however. It is a form of mock yawn which means she believes you are a pushover, or that you are boring her. Other face-touching signals should also be viewed as a warning. They are self-comfort gestures that normally signal discomfort, anxiety or boredom.

Lip-parting. The lips become fuller during sex, and any arousal or sexual interest can spark off this process, leading to subtle mouth-opening.

Pouting. A mouth gesture favoured by sex symbols. Combined with narrowed eyes and the head tilted back, *à la* Marilyn Monroe, it can simulate female orgasm. The origins of the pout owe less to sex and more to comfort, however – it mimics the child suckling at the breast. In women this can show a desire to be thought cute as well as sexy. In men it can reveal a desire to be mummied.

Shoulder-rubbing. In a man this can mean boredom. In a woman it can signal attraction if the rub is slow and sensual. The bare shoulder and upper arm are sensitive areas, and this gesture can be an invitation to touch. It also creates a barrier, though, with the arm crossing the chest. This makes it both sensual and self-protective. Be cautious. If it is combined with a forward lean that is not in your direction, the entire pose could be one of nervous or anxious self-protection.

Self-touch. In both men and women watch where the hands move when they are talking to you. Self-touch can be a sign to a prospective partner that this is where they would like to be touched by you. Watch especially for light, lingering touches to the mouth, ears, shoulders, wrists, breasts, chest, thighs and knees. Playing with jewellery that adorns any of these areas can be a displacement activity – in other words something that does virtually the same job. If the man is scratching his bum energetically, then forget what I have just said.

The following list of other phallic displays will sound about as subtle as a Benny Hill sketch, but you need to be warned, so here goes. In women, watch for any gestures that involve longish, cylindrical objects, like sucking fingers, lollipops, pens or spoons. Fondling pens lengthwise could be significant, as could fondling the stem of a wineglass, fingering its rim, sucking the froth off a cappuccino, licking the yoghurt off the lid of the pot, pushing a ring on and off a finger, eating a banana slowly, eating asparagus the proper way (with the fingers), putting on lipstick, and so on.

For men the list is shorter, unless the gestures are performed man to man, in which case most of the above list could apply. Man-to-woman gestures will often be less overt, although they will tend to border on the gross rather than being sensual. Most will involve the tie or a belt. Fiddling with cuffs or cuff links may reveal a desire to get naked. Playing with change in a trouser pocket can be the most obvious gesture, as it is as near as a man can get to fiddling with the penis itself in public. Often the gesture is performed at stressful moments, such as during a business presentation or when meeting someone for the first time, so it can also reveal a desire for self-comfort, as well as being a form of sexual advertising.

Beard, chin or nose-rubbing in a man can be phallic. A man's nose is quite a potent phallic symbol and rubbing it (especially at the fleshy tip) can be a signal of desire.

A man will often widen his stance when standing in front of a woman he likes. This accentuates the crotch display. If he is holding a drink he will often drop it to waist height or lower. When he talks to a woman he may even bounce up and down on his toes, which has the effect of simulating pelvic thrusting during sex.

Facial Expressions

Gaze. When we are attracted to someone we will watch their face closely to monitor their response to anything we have said. Close face-scanning, then, can signal attraction.

A held gaze is similarly a possible sign of attraction. Watch where the eyes move as they pass across your face. If someone is interested his or her eyes will stay on your face, even after eye contact has been broken. If the eyes move down to the mouth and then back up to the eyes, the attraction signal will be significantly stronger.

Not everyone is comfortable with sustained or even first-glance levels of eye contact. A traditional stance for the woman to take is to appear to repel the man's gaze by looking away in a childlike gesture of shyness. Often she will employ *less* eye contact overall with a man she fancies than with other people. This can be a flirt signal, or a sign of shyness brought on by her sense of attraction. (*However*, it can also be a sign of lack of interest. Be careful about how you interpret it. If a woman *is* attracted you can be sure that the gaze *will* return to the man's face again, fleetingly, several times, being averted again the moment it is reciprocated.)

When we are first attracted to someone it is natural to want to check out the rest of the body. Unfortunately, getting caught doing this can get a man accused of leering or ogling. So it will be done surreptitiously until the point that some sort of mutually acceptable attraction has been signalled, where-upon more open forms of body-watching can proceed. Look for face-watching that morphs into body-glance to signal interest.

Mirroring. This may well be the next response. It is a sign of empathy. Watch to see whether the other person responds to your changes of expression or movement through subconscious mimicry. It can occur at a distance as well as close up. It means they have a desire to be pleasing.

Feature-softening. When we see someone we like the whole face softens to become more attractive. Harsh lines tend to disappear and the eyes smile. People who are *attracted* will often become more *attractive* through this softening procedure, which will also make them look more youthful. When we fall in love our face is transformed when we look at the object of our affection. This is what Burt Bacharach referred to in a song as 'the look of love'. When a couple split the look dies, and the other person may well begin to look almost unfamiliar to us.

The suppressed smile. When someone is attracted to you they want to smile like a gurning idiot the moment they see you. In an attempt to play it cool, however, they may try to suppress the smile, but you can still see it start to develop.

The smile and head-tilt combo. This means a man is displaying his more childish, vulnerable side, looking for a reciprocal smile of approval. The head-tilt gesture is a visual question: 'Do you like me, then?'

Nodding. Obviously this gesture is a vital part of our non-sexual signalling. Look for rapt attention and increased nodding when you speak as a signal of attraction.

When men or women hunt in packs there are often more overt displays of body-watching, seen (by the pack) as less predatory and more light-hearted than solo ogling. These brazen signals of attraction are more to do with power than the mating process.

Touch

In the initial stages of a relationship people often look for excuses to touch as a prelude to more actively sexual touching. If a potential partner does any or all of the following you can begin to assume some interest:

- Touches or taps your arm as an emphatic gesture when speaking (or even taps your thigh).

- Moves a strand of hair away from your eyes.

- Puts a coat around your shoulders and then holds the shoulders for a moment.

- Touches your hand as you light his/her cigarette.

- Hits you playfully while laughing.

- Tickles you.

- Sits so close your legs touch.

- Holds your arm to direct you across the road.

- Whispers in your ear so that your faces touch.

From Social to Sexual

When we are in the first stages of a relationship, we run the gauntlet of look and touch, moving carefully through the gestures that could be labelled 'social' and on to the ones that can only be termed 'sexual'.

While we are in the 'social' stages we have the opportunity to back out if we need to. Once we veer into the sexual we use touch that cannot be disguised as anything else. Hand-holding, hugging, face-touching and even some forms of kissing (obviously not with tongues) can all be excused under the 'social' banner. The first touch gesture that crosses the boundary is body-touch.

Sometimes you meet someone in a formal situation, like the workplace, and the courtship rituals go on for weeks, months or even years (especially if one or both partners is married). Or you can meet someone socially and crash through the entire ritual in the space of an hour or less, moving from greeting to mating in as long as it takes you to get into the airline loo.

A complete leapfrogging of midway niceties, like flirting and social touching, is unusual, though. The speed at which you move will be dictated by your own preferences and the signals you receive from the other person.

Barriers

When we are in a comfortable relationship with someone our self-created barriers start to come down. After sex has occurred and the attraction and desire for more are mutual, there will be virtually no barriers between a couple. All arm-folding, mouth-covering and leg-crossing disappear, to be replaced by a desire to touch, hug and stare.

Such barriers will only reappear in a relationship when one or both of the partners lose their desire for sex with the other on either a temporary or a long-term basis. They may have a practical purpose – the couple might work together and need the barriers to ensure appropriate behaviour until they are alone again.

In the early stages barriers can be a signal of either shy attraction or a lack of interest, and so it is easy to confuse the messages. We employ many of the body-hug barriers to provide comfort when we feel anxious or nervous, which can easily be the case when we're in the company of someone we're attracted to. Look for add-on 'leakage' signals that accompany apparent barriers to try to discover the true meaning behind superficial rejection. *But* – know when to quit. If you're being signalled a clear lack of interest, clear off, don't be pushy and don't become a sex pest.

The following are common barriers:

Legs. Sitting with crossed legs is a comfortable and very common posture for women to adopt. If the top leg is turned away from you, though, a woman may be signalling lack of interest.

If a man crosses his legs, be more cautious. A more natural position for men is to have their legs spread-eagled. Crossed legs may be a deliberate barrier.

One leg laid across the top of the other, with the calf resting on the thigh, is likely to be a 'repel' barrier, especially if the top leg is being held.

Sitting on one leg is a listening or focusing gesture. Not overtly sexual, it is a semi-lotus position that implies a concentration that is intellectual rather than sexual.

Both legs folded underneath the torso is a youthful, uninhibited gesture that also presents a strong crotch display, especially if the hands are on the knees. However, it is a distance display rather than an invitation to touch. The body is taken away from, rather than extended towards, the person opposite.

Crossing the legs while standing is a rather quirky gesture that is quite common during the chat-up process. Superficially, it will usually imply a kind of gauche diffidence, the person you are speaking to making themselves less stable physically, or possibly shorter. On a deeper level, the crossing of the legs does rather imply that sexual access is denied, at least for the time being.

Knees. Holding the knees hugged to the chest is an almost complete barrier, implying the person is in need of comfort and love rather than sex. The legs from knee to ankle will hide almost the entire body.

Arms. Folded arms is the classic barrier, but does not always imply a desire to keep away from you. If the arm-fold is at the waist, a woman will be implying a desire for self-comfort that could involve you. The breasts are still displayed. This woman may be unhappy and want you to help, so be aware that there may be some counselling about a bad previous relationship to be undertaken before things go any farther.

If the arms are folded at chest height the barrier becomes more impenetrable. If the fold takes the form of a body-hug it is self-protective. If it is squared off and higher still, it may even look aggressive. In a man this gesture may be part of the chest-banging mating ritual, though. If one hand is free and touching the chin, the person could be displaying a desire to listen. If it is fiddling with a neck-chain the negative signals are stronger, though, implying anxiety or a sense of perceived threat behind the protective barrier.

Having the arms crossed while standing with the legs apart is a pose normally executed by men or rather butch women. Sexual access is there technically, but the folded arms imply 'Don't you dare!' This pose is aggressive and much loved by nightclub bouncers. You could be in for a rough night. You have been warned.

Legs *and* arms crossed should be seen as a warning sign. The other person is completely unreceptive to your chat-up. If the arms don't unfold during the small talk, consider yourself to have failed.

Straightening the tie, gripping the strap of a shoulder bag or finding any excuse to raise one or both arms when talking will all be means of creating a comfort barrier. If the other person does this as you approach, or while you are talking, be alert to the fact that they may feel uncomfortable. This could be caused by shyness, but you need to be alert to what might be negativity.

The goal-kick stance, otherwise known as the 'fig-leaf' pose, is a very obvious piece of barrier erection that probably needs no explanation. Performed solely by men, it involves standing with the hands cupped in front of the private parts. It rarely occurs when there are women around, but if it does consider yourself as being viewed with great fear by the man in question, who has spotted your potential as a one-woman castrator. This pose is normally used by men when they are talking to a group, as in a business presentation; however, it is not unknown as a social statement.

Fingers. Finger-steepling is a small but relatively serious barrier. If you are on the receiving end of a complete steeple, in which the hands are joined at the fingertips with the fingers pointing upwards, you can assume a pompous, calculating prat is monitoring you. If the fingers point towards you the other person may as well be pointing a metaphorical weapon in your direction. If the fingers are joined in a hand-clasp, the pose is more relaxed and less defensive, but the person is still making up their mind about you.

Mouth. Mouth-covering barriers are often a sign of a lack of sexual interest. The mouth is one of the key visual zones during all stages of attraction, so this barrier should never be ignored.

Gaze. If attraction is signalled by increased intensity of gaze, then lack of interest can equally well be signalled by a lack of eye contact or deliberate looking away. Shyness can also be a cause of this symptom, but never assume that this is the only explanation. One problem with being on the receiving end of negative eye contact from someone you fancy can be that you go out of your way to attract their attention, often increasing the frequency of your own eye contact until it becomes an inhibiting stare. This in turn will have the effect of making the other person look away even more.

Drinks. Watch any choreography with the glass. If it is raised as you approach or talk, and held at chest height or above, it is being used as a barrier to separate you. If the glass doesn't drop after a few minutes, give up. (Unless the woman is actively and suggestively running the tip of her finger around the rim, as mentioned earlier.) If the glass is held lower, but with both hands, the line of defence is still there. You can only hope that one hand will move away from the glass after a few moments. If the pose starts out quite open, but the glass starts to rise during your conversation, look for the nearest exit.

Objects. The workplace provides many objects that can be employed as body barriers, such as folders, books, documents, and so on. Many women potter around with a sheath of papers permanently glued to their chests. This can be due to lack of confidence or self-esteem, but it is hardly a mating call, either.

More generally, people will sometimes erect walls with objects. They stand behind chairs or tables, build a line of glasses or plates between you, or fill the intervening space with a handbag or a cushion. Look at the space between you and the person you like. Look at the size of that space, and what fills it. If there are objects between you, who put them there? Sometimes you can even see the other person pulling more props in, or rearranging them as the conversation continues.

Spectacles. Tinted glasses are one of my all-time pet hates. By choosing specs with tinted lenses, this person has decided to keep their distance from the rest of the world in a manner that looks distinctly dodgy. To bond with someone you need to be able to read the messages coming from their eyes. Even slight tints will create a big barrier, then (although you shouldn't take it personally, as they obviously wore the ghastly appendages before you appeared on the scene).

Sunglasses are different. They can be put on or taken off as the mood dictates. They will be a very strong barrier to any approach, but the messages can be more subtle and complex than you might suppose, and not necessarily a signal to clear off and die. Many women use shades in the same way they used fans a couple of centuries ago, to conceal the fact that they are watching you closely, a sure sign of attraction in most circumstances.

If you are being monitored through clear spectacles the only assumption you should make is that the man or woman in question has dodgy eyesight. If, however, you are on the receiving end of the 'peering over the top of the specs' routine, then the message may be negative. The fact that this person prefers to keep their reading glasses in place while talking or listening to you suggests the time they have spare to be interested in you is severely limited.

Open Body Language

Open gestures are often seen as a sign of honesty and a desire to communicate, and very often they are. If the person you have approached keeps within the socially prescribed distance, with open gestures and the occasional emphatic hand movement, you can assume that they are happy to talk. 'Comfortable' levels of eye contact will also signal an amber/green light. The other sign of approval will be that old favourite, the smile.

Smiling is a non-attack gesture. When we meet a stranger under normal circumstances we feel a sense of relief when they smile at us. If the smile looks genuine we assume we are not in any danger. If the smile looks 'stretched' and fake, though, we may still flinch. Animals tend to bare their teeth before an attack, and your receptors may well be warning you of impending danger.

By opening your mouth in this way you reveal a very vulnerable part of your anatomy, which is why the smiler will often expect a smile in return. In a way it will be a mutual signal of peace. As the conversation goes on, the smile is used to signal approval and empathy. Monitoring the other person's smile rate is important if you want to gauge how attractive you are to them. Consider:

- Does the smile look congruent or false?

- Does it come at appropriate moments in the conversation, or is it being used as a polite gesture only?

• Has the smile rate increased since you started talking?

• Does this person look into your eyes and then smile? (If so, you can get your solicitor to draw up the pre-nuptial agreement.)

If the body language appears too open, hold back and take stock. Men, in particular, have a habit of sitting back in a seat with their legs apart and a hand behind their head. This position could signal that they are too relaxed, though. Ditto an open-looking slump in a seat. When a man fancies a woman you should expect more preening gestures, with a positive alteration in posture. If a man slumps back you can either assume he's not prepared to try or he's expecting the woman to make all the running, which suggests arrogance.

Engineering Signals

There may come a time during an interaction when you want a little added motivation either to stay the course or advance. This is when you can engineer a response. It's a bit like wetting a finger to see which way the wind's blowing. You can:

• Speak a little more quietly. If the other person likes you they will use the opportunity to come closer to hear what you are saying. If they stand their ground and say 'Pardon?' you should start to worry. If they stand their ground and pretend to have heard what you said you should start to get depressed.

• Pretend you can't hear what they are saying. If the room is noisy this gives the other person a perfect opportunity to lean even closer and speak right into your ear. They can even touch you to do so. If they just shout louder, call it a day.

• Ask for a light. Very Bette Davis and very long-term health problems, but, again, an opportunity for the other person to touch your hand as they light your fag. If they chuck you the matches you've got the red card.

• Ask to taste their drink/food. If they watch as you do so you're in with a chance because they will be using the opportunity to catch you with your mouth open and something in it. If they look away as you eat or sip you can assume they're not interested. (I'm sure you don't need to be told only to do this with someone you've been introduced to. Never make such a request of a stranger.)

- Place your glass on the table/bar and see where they put their own. If it is next to yours things are looking hopeful.

- Leave a small crumb on your face and see whether they wipe it away.

- Similarly, allow a strand of hair to stray across your face.

- Allow a small silence, then laugh out loud and see whether they laugh too.

- Pop to the loo, then peek out to see whether they're watching for your return or checking their appearance while you're gone.

And there's always the anti-flirting technique, in which you turn the flirting off for a while, lower your head, stop smiling or look away (see the chapter on making yourself desirable). If he/she is not interested this will produce no reaction – they may even look away or fall silent as well. If he/she is keen you should expect to see signals to the effect that they want you to reboot the niceness. They may even start flirting with you to elicit a more positive response.

Greeting Signals

The British are becoming less formal in their methods of greeting people and – although they still have a way to go to catch up with the US – they are beginning to signal more through conscious and subconscious leakage during this key moment in a transaction.

As usual, much of the impact has been scuppered by business-based techniques and training, which have blurred the boundaries between the genuine and the faux. Sales people are often taught to use handshakes and other greetings to imply instant friendship, while people in more theatrical professions will grip complete strangers in heartfelt hugs that would make a grizzly blush.

So can you gauge attraction by the type of greeting you receive? Often you can. We all use small, give-away signs that will signal potential differences in relationships as we greet people.

The no-touch greeting

This needn't signal a lack of interest. A handshake is a formal greeting signal and so may not be used socially, especially among young people and drunks. If you are being introduced for the first time, look for that classic first sign of interest – the prolonged glance. If there is interest there your eyes should meet at this point.

If someone shakes hands with everyone but you there is no need to be paranoid. Many men are still not sure whether or not to shake hands with a woman. Or the hesitation could be due to shyness. I doubt it is due to the fact that you are too revolting to touch.

The handshake

If someone is attracted to you they are unlikely to produce more than the formal handshake on being introduced, albeit accompanied by the meaningful glance. If you know the person quite well but they are still sticking at the handshake stage, and the greetings are not in an office environment, you can assume you are being kept at arm's length.

If the handshake contains any 'Hey, we're friends' add-ons, like the your-hand-in-both-of-mine hand sandwich, or the arm touch or elbow grab, you shouldn't get too excited. These techniques denote closer relationships in the US, but in the UK they often only convey a fake bonhomie.

One of the best examples of a 'give-away' handshake in living memory was the famous shot of Princess Diana shaking hands with James Hewitt while presenting him with a polo cup. While he leans forward slightly, looking her straight in the eye, she looks away and giggles. If you shake hands with someone and they look away laughing in this way, you can assume they fancy you.

The cheek kiss

If this is performed as an air kiss, with restraining shoulder grip, read nothing into it. If the cheeks touch there should be some electricity, because cheek-to-cheek or any head-to-head touching is extremely intimate. If the bodies touch and her lips brush his cheek then the whole thing is a lot more intimate.

Look for any denial gestures after the event. When we want to downplay a gesture we will often tack one of these on afterwards. With the cheek kiss it may come with an after-pat – signalling rejection after the event – or a quick turning away.

The hug

The same will be true of the hug. If it is non-sexual the pelvic area will be carefully held back. If bodies touch along their length you can consider that intimacy is intended. The denial gesture to look for here, though, is excessive back-patting, an aggressive signal intended to eliminate any suggestion of intimacy.

If someone likes you they will move towards you whatever the greeting. Look for any 'secret' signalling. With the hug or cheek kiss this will be a small extra squeeze, usually of the arm or shoulder. If you get a small extra squeeze in a formal handshake you have probably encountered a freemason or a pervert.

Boredom Check

Watch out for the following signs, which may indicate boredom on the part of the person you're talking to:

- They reflect too long before they speak.

- Their laughter seems false. The smile doesn't reach the eyes and is non-symmetrical or 'stretched'.

- The laugh response is identical each time and looks rehearsed. A real laugh involves the eyes, neck and diaphragm.

- Their eyes keep flitting over your shoulder.

- They glance at their watch.

- They greet other people in the room, or turn their torso away from you to give them broader access to the room.

- They take a long breath.

- They stifle a yawn.

- Their posture is slumped.

- They have a blank facial expression, or respond late to what you say.

- They nod rapidly, signalling a desire to interrupt.

- They tap their foot or finger increasingly fast.

- They shift about.

- Their responses are overblown.

As I've said throughout this book, body language is not a precise science. When you decode the incoming signals you should only ever believe that you are reading between the lines. Visual signals allow us to make an educated guess regarding a person's inner feelings, but this can often be wildly inaccurate. If you see none of the 'attraction' indicators listed above, you might as well count yourself out of the action. And if you witness any or all of them you should only ever interpret them as an amber rather than a green light.

CHAPTER ELEVEN

Creating Empathy and Rapport

It would be much too crude to say that people come in certain behavioural 'types'. Most of us are far too complex to pigeon-hole, and to try to do so would be dangerous. When we attach labels to other people we begin to typecast them. This is why the process used by most dating agencies is so flawed. Once you have answered 'yes' or 'no' to their many questions you have begun to close the door on the alternatives. Yet in reality our 'type' varies in each and every transaction.

The skill involved in creating the kind of empathy and rapport that will boost your chances of starting and maintaining a successful relationship depends on your ability to form a behavioural 'match'. For this 'match' to be effective you will need to be flexible. Remember: humans are complex. Many of our behavioural techniques are responses to the behaviour of others, which is why you should take everyone you meet at face value. When someone describes a person in terms of their behavioural 'type' to you they are really only describing the behaviour that their own transaction elicited.

To appeal to someone else your behaviour should be comple-mentary to his or hers. Remember the theory of rewarded behaviour. Their actions are intended to elicit a certain type of response. If they get what they are looking for the transaction has been complementary. But – as anyone who has children will tell you – what you look for isn't always what you *want*. A naughty, demanding child might appear to be happy if it is given what it is asking for. But what it gains in the short term may lead to a long-term loss – if the parent gives in easily the child may start to feel insecure, owing to a lack of overall parental control.

To describe this in relationship terms, one partner may display dominant characteristics while the other may adopt a more passive stance to form what will appear to be a complementary 'match'. Aggressive or critical behaviour usually seeks submissive responses to secure a complementary transaction. But this combination may not work so readily in reality in that it may not be what both partners actually *want*. I have seen men with doormat wives who have left them for someone far more assertive.

To create successful rapport, then, you will have to use something that boxers call the 'duck and dive' routine. Judge your partner's behaviour without prejudice. Allow for the fact that you will get a turn to fulfil your own needs. Creating rapport by modifying your behaviour on first meeting is one thing, but spending a lifetime trying to provide a perfect 'match' to someone else is another. What you need to do for short-term success – namely, instant attraction – is to supply a short burst of complementary transactions. Then, if the relationship becomes long-term, you need to work out a series of acceptable 'behaviour and reward' techniques that give each of you a turn at being rewarded if you aren't always truly compatible. This give-and-take is vital to the success of a permanent relationship. Without it the double act will misfire constantly, or one partner will be in a permanent state of submission to the other, which will lead to resentment.

Quick Hits

To create instant rapport in casual encounters you can use the mirroring technique that I have mentioned before, by subtly copying the other person's body signals. In longer-standing relationships or partnerships, though, you will need to delve deeper into the bag of psychological tricks.

Whatever the other person's verbal style, it is worth noting their physical presentation and behaviour. Their gestures, posture and expressions will give you clues as to their preferred behaviour. Once you have established what it is you can begin to tailor your own body language behaviour so that it is complementary to theirs. Or – and you'll hate me for confusing you further on this one, but I never said it was going to be easy, did I? – you can take your life in your hands and try to alter their behavioural state, using your own style of signalling.

For example, imagine you have just met someone who is displaying signals of dominant behaviour. If you like this person you have several choices. First, you can undertake a complementary transaction, whether short- or long-term. This would entail you giving this person the response they are seeking – namely, a passive one. This may well lead to a conflict-free relationship – *unless* you get fed up playing the doormat. If you are keen to play the downtrodden husband or wife for a lifetime, then go ahead. (Many people do and it can work a treat.)

Or you can decide to do the opposite and hope the other person changes his/her behavioural style accordingly. This would entail you responding to the dominant stimulus by displaying dominant behaviour of your own. This is, of course, taking more of a risk, but hey, who said the path of true love would ever run smoothly? If this other person is the type who has been waiting for a strong person to stand up to him/her you may be able to strike a bargain. If not, you will clash from the word go and probably not even get to the first date.

Alternatively, you could present in a complementary style in the initial stages and then morph gradually into something a lot more assertive. Your potential partner will choose either fight, flight or surrender.

At this point you are thinking: 'But isn't it better if I just act myself?'

No one can be themselves until they have found out exactly who that self is. The only 'yourself' you know at present is what is left when you can't be faffed to make much of an effort. There's nothing wrong with tactics.

Sometimes you will need to play this game for a lifetime, but it could be something you switch on and off depending on mood or circumstance. Either way, you will need to read your partner first before deciding which angle to take.

By way of illustration, a colleague of mine married a man

who presented as a tough corporate cookie in business. By the time he got home he would appear to be all out of 'hard man' and would revert to childlike displays, like stealing food while she was cooking or playing other little games and pranks. (And if this sounds nauseating to you then I have to say it worked, because he was industrial-strength cute.) My friend decided to adopt complementary behaviour, acting like a mummy and generally treating him like a child. It appeared to work and they still seem happy. My friend is not totally into the role but it keeps him content, and when she needs parenting he is there for her. It's less rewarding for guests, though, as watching a grown man root through kitchen cupboards to find where the 'choccies' are hidden can bring on an attack of projectile vomit. Nevertheless, they're good fun as a couple in many other ways.

If this type of long-term project puts you off, work on modifying short-term responses to get the best out of a relationship, from first meeting to last will and testament time. You can use the technique as a trick to attract or as part of your effort at making a more permanent relationship work.

Monitoring your partner's changing moods and adapting your response accordingly can create an attractive symmetry in a relationship. Study the following body language behaviour guide to discover from the displayed signals you are being sent which type your potential partner is presenting as.

Dominant male

- Makes full use of his height.

- Holds head high.

- Goes in for periods of intense eye contact with eyes fully open, punctuated by periods of looking about the room at other people.

- Moves his eyes from your eyes to other parts of your face, as though distracted, while you talk.

- Displays close spatial behaviour.

- Tends to place his hands on his hips, or use other body-bulking physical displays.

- Spreads his legs wide.

- Uses stretching movements or gestures that tend to enclose you.

- Rocks back and forth on toes.

- Stands in front of you.

- Laughs at you when you speak, even though you aren't trying to be funny.

- Follows traditional etiquette, such as holding doors open or helping you on with your coat.

- Moves things that belong to you, such as picking your bag up from the floor and putting it on a chair.

- Places his hands on his thighs when sitting, with the thumb on the outside of the leg and elbows raised.

- Sits with legs spread wide, feet stretched out.

- Will have one hand on his hip while the other rubs his chin.

- Folds arms quite high on chest.

- Tilts head with one eyebrow raised.

- Puffs his chest out.

- His hand will be on top in a hand-clasp.

- Walks in front of you.

- Puts his arm around your shoulders when walking.

In sexual terms the dominant male is often keen to self-touch or self-display, particularly as regards the crotch area – for example, sitting back with his legs apart. He may instigate touch directed towards your sexual areas, such as thigh-patting or hugging. He will either take the initiative physically or lay back and be verbally demanding.

Submissive female

- Holds chin low.

- Eye contact is evasive.

- Smiles excessively.

- Nods excessively.

- Leans towards you to catch every word.

- Displays signs of self-checking – small touches to hair, clothing, etc.

- Utters a quick, nervous laugh at end of own speech, maintaining eye contact, encouraging you to smile.

- Raises eyebrows.

- Smiles without showing teeth.

- Suppresses the smile, dropping her head.

- Displays incongruent mirroring.

- Uses palm-up gestures.

- Engages in 'performance' speaking – using expression and gestures while talking but 'packing them away' again quickly when finished.

- Gestures with the hands at shoulder height or higher

- Uses self-embrace arm gestures.

- Makes 'checking' touch gestures that follow your eye movement, e.g. you look at her nose and she touches it a second or so later.

Sex is not usually instigated by the submissive female. In response terms she may display nervous, diffident signals but then submit quickly and quietly.

Dominant female

- Maintains prolonged eye contact with little softening of the eyes.

- Uses little or no mirroring – all gestures and expressions driven by own emotions.

- Presents squared shoulders and straight neck.

- Breasts are pushed out towards you.

- Legs are straight when standing, never one knee bent or angled pelvis.

- Uses finger-baton or pointing signals when talking.

- Employs self-indicating gestures while talking, like patting own body or pointing at self.

- Gives open-mouthed smile showing both rows of teeth.

- Tilts head back when laughing.

- Upper arms are held away from body.

- Uses hair or head-touches to display soft skin on underneath of upper or lower arm.

- Crosses legs with the leg on top swinging quite quickly.

- Raises one eyebrow.

- Looks over top of glasses.

- Taps or pats you playfully.

- Ruffles your hair.

The dominant female will instigate sex quickly, having offered lots of physical hints, often on first meeting. Eye contact will increase as advances are made. She is quick to touch, especially the predatory touch that 'sprays the territory', warning off any other females.

Submissive male

- Has a stooped posture.

- Puts hands in pockets.

- Shrugs when talks.

- Shakes head when talks.

- Uses the downturned mouth shrug.

- Folds arms in body hug.

- Is animated and playful when criticising self.

- Watches faces for signs of approval.

- Employs contrasting postures, as though realigning after self-policing.

- Responds quickly and rather nervously when you move.

- Puts arm around your waist.

- His hand will be underneath in hand-clasp.

- Wrings hands.

- Makes playful gestures or statements followed by a nervous laugh and face-checking.

In sexual terms the submissive male is happy to do as he is told, tiresomely unable to instigate new ideas or demands.

Nurturer

- Uses eye contact with very softened eyes.

- Grooms you, flicking dust off clothing or smoothing hair (will also be predatory and/or territorial, although much nurturing behaviour can be both).

- Ducks head and smiles into your face.

- Uses reassuring touches, like hand-patting or back-rubbing.

- Goes in for lots of face-watching, but side-on rather than full-frontal.

- Smiles out of sympathy rather than humour.

- Nods slowly while listening, to affirm emotion rather than understanding of overall message.

- Uses lots of slow, careful self-comfort touches, like hair-stroking or hand-rubbing.

With the nurturer, each sexual advance will be punctuated by 'checking' gestures, to see whether you're OK. The approach will be slow: lots of face-touching, back-rubbing, stroking, and so on. He or she may massage your shoulders, and will certainly run off for tissues and light cigarettes afterwards.

Free child

- Gestures used to display emotion, often emphatic; reactive gestures often very open and exaggerated.

- Has wide eyes and raised brows.

- Smile is puckered.

- Takes large strides, in a bouncing walk.

- Will run if hurrying.

- Uses lots of impatient gestures: tapping, bouncing, looking about distracted, glancing at watch.

- 'Plays' with objects.

- Leans back, slumped, in seat.

- Nods quickly.

- Belly-laughs, falling forward in seat and clutching stomach.

The free child will instigate sex through play and hint, usually starting with tickling, fun hugging or even mock fighting. He or she will laugh a lot before and during, and will use childish names for body parts.

Adult

- Maintains confident eye contact.

- Uses open but not flamboyant gestures that either illustrate or emphasise words.

- Has a confident social smile.

- Uses facial expressions that respond appropriately to your words.

- Employs mirroring techniques.

The adult makes confident hints about sex, and is not afraid to touch, whether in a sexual or a non-sexual context, eyes scanning your face and body. Intentions are open, but no inappropriate advances are made.

Remember that these states can be transient, and that your partner might move from one to another throughout your relationship, or even during one session of sex. Often when we move into one of these states we will subconsciously display some or all of the above behaviours to signal our mood. When we do this we are 'asking' the other person to perform in a complementary way – we want them to play ball. Dominant will seek out submissive, adult will look for adult, and the free child will seek either nurture or dominance, depending on how naughty they intend to be.

You can instigate or even maintain your relationship by matching states accordingly. Alternatively, you may want to instigate change. This would mean meeting dominant with dominant, or with adult.

Does this work? It can do, if it creates some sort of change in the other person's behaviour, and if they themselves are happy with that change. In family relationships this type of tailoring is vital for continuity. As we have seen, if a child throws a tantrum it is looking for submission from its parent. If the parent gives it what it wants the transaction will have worked, but the child is rewarded for its bad behaviour. To break the cycle the transaction needs to not work, so that the child learns that the tantrum is ineffective and tries another – hopefully more socially appropriate – tactic.

But a family already has a bond that is virtually continual. When you find a new partner there is – initially – little if any pressure for the relationship to develop. If you don't form a behaviour 'match' you will need to have an excess of other forms of compatibility. So you either:

- Create a match during the early stages and work on the corrective stuff later.

- Perform in your preferred style and see what happens.

- Create a match and stick with it throughout your life together.

Maintaining Balance

The true test of any relationship is the ability of the two people in it to adapt their behaviour styles to get the best out of every moment. Sadly, as a relationship progresses one or both parties will often start to get lazy or to take the other person so much for granted that they can't be bothered any longer. The more conflict is produced by this apathy, the more resentment will grow until you become completely unwilling to adapt to any situation. This is when you begin to develop patterns of dysfunctional behaviour that neither of you likes and yet which neither of you will break because you feel you will lose face if you do so.

Breaking existing patterns by changing your behaviour and responses to certain stimuli is relatively easy. The only person stopping you is you. Remember the phrase: *If I always do what I've always done then I'll always get what I've always got.*

To create change you need to create a hiatus. Even a pause of a second following a particular stimulus can be enough time to remind you to respond thoughtfully, not to react instinctively. Plan a different tactic. Create a new response. The change needn't be large or traumatic, as long as it is some kind of shift in behaviour.

This change of tactics will help create a much healthier long-term relationship. Many of these patterns are created during the dating stages, which is why I mention them here.

As I have said, adapting your style to complement your partner's is often a clever technique for attracting them in the first place. This is really only akin to wearing a smart suit to a job interview. But once the suggestion of something more long-term looms on the horizon you will need to think of more constructive techniques. This should not entail sudden dramatic changes of behaviour that will alarm your new partner and suggest you were only acting during your first few dates. Nor should it ever lead to a complete bottoming-out of behaviour, to the point where you are so into 'being yourself' that you slob out in a baggy tracksuit, farting and burping at will.

Many relationship books endorse the 'keep the act going until you drop' style of relationship maintenance, where you fill the house with fresh flowers and scented candles for your partner's return each evening and employ Jerry Hall's mother's dictum of being a maid in the living room, a cook in the kitchen and a whore in the bedroom. (Personally I would be more in favour of a slut in the kitchen and a whore in the bedroom, but then who am I to talk?)

Now I would like to change your thinking a little on the non-verbal messages you send out to and receive from your partner from the first date onward.

Rule 1: Use your eyes

Watch your partner. Never, ever stop monitoring them for mood and behavioural changes. Short of climbing inside their head it is the only way to read their mind. Know when they are being playful, sensitive, sensual or serious. Look for the signs because they are always there. A mother learns to read her child's mind and she is able to do so because she learns to read its body language signals. It's not hard. If you are in a long-term relationship you will have ample time for study. *Just keep looking.*

Rule 2: Assume the best and the worst

As a general rule of thumb, most men are quite simplistic in their relationship thinking. Women, on the other hand, can be complex. This may cause problems when a woman assumes that a man is thinking in the same complex way as she is. If you are a woman, imagine yourself to be playing a game of chess in which you are planning ten moves ahead and your man is focused only on the next one. I know all this is breath-takingly simplistic and riddled with stereotypical assumptions, but just try using it as a theory for a while and I think you'll see it works. Consider any relationship problem you like in terms of this assumption and I bet you it will unravel. For example:

'Why did he chat up/sleep with that woman when he knew it would damage our relationship?' (Well, when he met her the only move he was focused on was getting her into bed. What happened after that was not part of the equation. The fact that he is now distraught that it has caused damage is also genuine. You are now his current focus.)

'Why did he bother asking me out when he had no intention of turning up?' (Two possible reasons: asking you out was genuinely what he wanted to do *at the time*; or he asked only because he could see it was what you wanted him to do. Once you were off the scene the pressure was off, too. He feels he did what you wanted, and so you should be grateful.)

'Why did he say he'd call? Why not just let me know he wasn't interested?' (Think time zones again. It was the *right* thing to say *at the time*. It was what you wanted. Whether or not actually to make the call was an unrelated decision.)

'Why did he tell so many lies?' (His choices were simple – either to do something that he shouldn't and then lie about it in order not to hurt you and cause a scene, or not to do that naughty fun thing. Think simply: which makes the most sense?)

Men, on the other hand, believe they can ask a woman a simple question and get a straight answer in reply. They are constantly confused and traumatised when complexity is the result. They may lie but they do not understand deviousness. It gives them brain-ache. Time and time again they ask simple questions, never learning the sheer stupidity of this behaviour. For example:

'What do you want for your birthday?' (If you have to ask, it means you don't understand me. Just go out and get something perfect.)

'What's wrong with just giving you money so you can choose for yourself?' (It is blatantly unromantic. The effort of shopping and choosing is part of the act of love.)

'What's wrong with this tie, then?' (Don't ask. Don't argue. Just take it off and burn it.)

'I thought you said you didn't mind if I got home late. You said don't rush.' (Getting back at 2 a.m. is not the same as 'not rushing'.)

The rule applies also to non-verbal communications. Work on the sweeping assumption that what men are displaying through their body language signals is pretty much what they are feeling. If they are acting indifferent they probably are indifferent. If they are acting like a kid they probably want to be treated like one.

Men need to work on the assumption that most women have usually got many more issues going on than those they are displaying. We are talking tip of a very big iceberg here. Look at the surface signals and read them as just the presenting symptoms of something far greater and more complex. Be afraid. We expect you to dig. Dig about with a man and you will probably close him down. Dig about nicely with a woman and she will assume you care enough to try to understand.

This contrast of styles can lead to confusion or conflict, but only if you judge by your own standards and values.

The World Map Theory

Ever seen a foreign map of the world? The thing looks almost unrecognisable. Then you notice why. Great Britain is not in the middle. That only happens on a British map of the world. You probably thought, like me, that the map we grew up with was *the* map of the world, but it isn't, it's only ours. To understand your partner you need to work to his/her values, and therefore his/her map of the world. Because it's different this doesn't mean it's wrong. Never judge it by your own map. You might find reference points you can share, but you will also discover vast differences. It's easier to work with them than change them. The best relationships happen when some reference points are changed to allow the relationship to develop and some left alone because they are vital to the individual. When we start a new relationship we often want to be two halves of the same whole. New couples often act the same, speak the same and even dress the same for a while. This is cute, but it will ultimately work against them if they pretend to be twins. When this occurs any separateness will be seen as disloyalty, which it isn't.

Bodytalk – the Dating Stages

Reading your man

Take most of what is presented to you at face value. Men *do* mask with their body language but they mainly do so to appear less nervous or softer than they are. Trying to see behind the mask is not useful. What they hide they don't want you to see.

Try to watch without staring. Men get paranoid when you look at them too much.

Monitor the different facets of your partner and take them at face value. Most men are put under pressure from birth to be in turn tough, funny, brave, childish, laddish, manly, sporty, businesslike and even 'in touch with their feminine side'. What you see displayed will be a succession of any or most of these facets. Treat him like a multiple personality disorder and respond to each facet without prejudice and without reference to previous ones. It is pointless tailoring your body language responses to a previous facet and then arguing when it doesn't work. What you see is what you get and what you need to work with. Pointing out any change will be deemed rude.

Reward the positive behaviours by creating a match and try to ignore the negatives. Rewarded behaviour tends to recur. Be careful that you aren't unwittingly rewarding negative behaviour, though. What you see as punishment may well be the response he was trying to evoke. This can happen with arguments, which are often ended with passionate making-up sessions. Creating conflict can then be seen as a positive device to evoke the intense levels of passion. If you hate the conflict, then watch how you behave afterwards.

Never assume that each date will be the same, or that your relationship will make any sense chronologically. Men don't tend to build a relationship as if drawing an upward slope on a graph. They can go from a high peak straight to a middle or a low without a murmur. Monitor the body language signals on each and every date and react accordingly. Avoid reference to the previous date and advances made there. Take every moment at face value. The man you had sex with on the last outing might well act like a stranger on the next. Try to avoid seeing this as a problem or reading too much into it. That was then, this is now. Keep that as your mantra and you won't go far wrong.

Reading your woman

Take little of what you see at face value, but never draw the conclusion that she is being deliberately unpleasant. Women communicate on many different levels at once, and this can prove unsettling until you understand the technique. Avoid responding to the body language you see on display. Always assume there is more going on. Women like to 'test' their men with this routine. The idea is that – if you really care – you will know what we want or what we need without asking. Asking is cheating and will never receive a positive response because – as you have surely been told before – 'If I have to tell you then there's no point'.

Gird your loins and be direct when you sense trouble brewing. If you ignore what looks like a long face you will find the negative behaviour increases until it is impossible to ignore. Indulge in a spot of undivided attention. Sit down, use eye contact, even take the woman's hand, and ask: 'What's wrong?' Do *not* do this, though, if what is wrong is you, and very obviously so. Asking what's wrong when you have just been caught snogging another woman is foolish to the point of idiocy. In this kind of situation you will need to apologise. Again, use the undivided attention routine with your body language – eye contact, nodding and facial responses. *Don't* look away once, not even if the room blows up or a streaker runs past.

If you have to lie to your woman, do it by e-mail. Women *always* know when you're telling a lie. Your body language flags it up a mile off, and I'm not going to tell you how for obvious reasons. If the lie appears to have worked it is only because we have decided not to cause a scene. You also need to remember that we never, ever forget, and only very, very rarely forgive. Only your mummy ever provided unconditional love.

Never buy flowers after a row or to say 'sorry'. Women see flowers as a celebratory gesture that proves we are loved and cherished. The reason we avoid binning them when they are bought as an apology is that we hate to destroy anything living. Money is a better way to apologise, believe me. Otherwise do it verbally and through your body language. Practise in the mirror until you can utter an apology and look as though you mean it. And never start laughing once it has been accepted.

Never ruffle a woman's hair, or hug her when she is dressed up, or try to kiss her when she is wearing lipstick, unless it's the end of the evening and you are going to have sex and get messy anyway. (David Beckham offered the perfect solution to this when he kissed Victoria on the end of her nose, a shot that was featured in most tabloids around the time of their wedding. The gesture is at once cute, romantic and thoughtful.)

Creating Rapport with the Pack

At some stage in the meeting–dating–mating ritual you will be asked to meet up with your partner's friends and family. Often you meet the friends before the parents.

These meetings should be seen as key points in the relationship. If you are older you might find yourself being introduced to your partner's children, too. Acceptance is vital but difficult.

Forewarned is forearmed. Find out who your partner was last married to/dating. Never assume that this person was Mr/Miss Popularity among the pack, although there is a good chance they were. Unearth as many of the details as you can without getting or sounding paranoid.

If the pack is well bonded you need to understand that you will upset the balance somewhat. They might feel threatened on all sorts of levels – by your age, your attractiveness or the fact that you might steal their pal/baby away from them.

Do:

- Look friendly when you meet, but don't be pushy.

- Watch before jumping in.

- Talk to them individually.

- Discover who is the alpha male/female in the pack quite early on. The key to acceptance may lie with them.

- Ask about your partner. Bow to their greater authority and experience.

- Join in and mirror as much as possible.

Don't:

- Cling to your partner like a limpet.

- Slag your partner off or talk in a derogatory way about him/her.

- Use sexual bonding gestures towards your partner.

- Look as if you indulge in private conversations or shared jokes.

- Flirt your way around the group.

- Be loud.

- Hug them all straight away.

Long-term Relationships

Avoid the usual advice about romantic set pieces, such as having a candlelit supper ready when your partner comes home from work or going off on romantic weekends. These events have an air of preconception about them, a bit like New Year's Eve, when you know you are going to *have* to have fun. They also imply you're not doing well the rest of the time and need to scrub up properly now and again. Keep in mind that most people work long hours these days, and are often knackered when they get home from work. Imagine the horror of getting home, looking forward to a foot spa and a cup of Earl Grey, to find Barry White on the sound system and your husband draped across the kitchen table clad only in a PVC thong.

If you want to make things work, go for continuous improvement. Look good at all times, but in different ways. There are look-good lounging clothes and look-good dress-ups. No woman has to swan around in lace and pearls all the time, and no man is expected to live in a freshly ironed shirt and lace-up shoes. Ditto with your body language. You can relax but still look attractive. Establish your body language bottom line and strive not to go below it. Do this for yourself as much as for your partner.

Never make assumptions about your partner. Be perceptive no matter how well you think you know them. People change. Jobs change us, children change us, life changes us, and age changes us. Getting older is no more a straight-slope option than a developing relationship. Ageing can be depressing to some and comfortable to others. Many of us fight it all the way, and this can lead to crazy behaviour around middle age. The belief that you are in the Last Chance Saloon can cause outbreaks of adolescentitis that might mystify someone who is already into the world of Saga holidays and Damart underwear while their partner is prancing round to Eminem and having their navel pierced. Try to keep in tune with this madness, even if you don't understand it. Change your own bodytalk. Keep in step. The big slipper stuff will kick in eventually; meanwhile you might share some fun en route.

Be respectful. I know this sounds very wholesome-American, but it is a necessary aspect of your body language if you want to develop a sound relationship. Listen when your partner talks to you and never, ever stop sending out signals to show you are listening. Use eye contact and appropriate facial expressions. Keep adopting the 'look of love' when you are with your partner. Soften the eyes, soften the expression and remember to transform yourself. The face you show your partner should be a face you show nobody else. Never allow the eyes to go dead. Always avoid signals of irritation. If you need to get irritated, do so through words, not deeds. The sight of that facial expression will stay with your partner for ever, but a few words will fade with time, unless they include 'divorce' or 'kill'.

Give undivided attention regularly.

Use touch regularly. A small touch as you leave the room or arrive home or walk past one another makes a huge impact. Don't just go for sexual touch, kissing or hugging. Face- or hand-touching, hair- or shoulder-stroking can be equally high-impact. These take little effort but keep the warmth alive.

CHAPTER TWELVE

The Science of Dress

Clothes are more than just fashion items or body covering. The garments you choose to present yourself in form part of your non-verbal display and tell a potential partner what you feel about yourself, your status and your sexuality.

All garments have their own signals. No outfit says nothing. The least you can say is that you are a member of a certain pack or tribe. The City business suit is worn for exactly this reason. Its bland, sober colouring and traditional lines tell people little about the wearer's individuality but a lot about pack membership. Dressing like the rest of the group is a little like wearing school uniform.

Your clothes have five main 'messaging' functions. They will display:

1. Group or tribal connections
2. Status or aspirational status
3. Inner self-esteem and confidence
4. Personality
5. Sexuality

Over the past few decades it has been women who have led the field in industrial-strength grooming and clothing displays, but now all this is changing. The new generation of young single men are being encouraged by fashion and market pressure to spend as long if not longer on their appearance. David Beckham, a current UK role model, is regarded as being more high-maintenance than his wife in terms of hairstyle and fashion sense.

So how can you ensure you talk the right language to attract and keep your ideal mate?

With normal body language it is difficult to isolate one gesture or facial expression and hold it up for scrutiny without seeing it in context. A pointing finger is notoriously aggressive, but if it is done with a laugh the negative implications can be nullified. The correct way to read any signal is by seeing it as part of a cluster of signals. Place it in context and you begin to get a clearer picture.

The same is true of clothing. Some garments scream their message, while others signal more subtly. Others can even negate some messages. Current fashion is notorious in this department, with a very pick-and-mix approach to things like short skirts, bare midriffs, body piercing and tattoos. Historically this overall look would probably have been a signal for a hooker, but times change and so do attitudes. A couple of years ago the look on the catwalks was called 'Heroin Chic', with skinny, pale-skinned models trying to ape the look of heroin addicts. Part of fashion's role is to shock. The problem that arises socially is that not everyone understands the connotations. A recent look for men involved the return of the knitted tank top, a garment that has always been a safe bet as a signal for a grade-A nerd or mummy's boy. So when your bloke arrives with one on the first date, how can you tell if he's being old fashioned and pervy or cool and ironic?

Most partnership dress messages involve three quite separate relationship stages:

1. What you wear to attract on first meeting
2. What you wear to date
3. What you wear when you live together

First Meeting

The clothes you wear when you first meet your potential partner will do much to create a 'match' in his/her eyes – or not.

Do you fit into this person's pack? Do you wear the right sort of uniform? The younger you are the stronger the pressure may be to create congruence with the rest of his/her peers. The stronger the pack or tribe, the bigger the danger from looking like a 'loner'. Uniform dressing of whatever kind will also signal security and fast-track rapport. If you want to pass the first hurdle it is helpful to dress in the same group style as the person you like.

It is also true that opposites attract, and that some people will find the loner or oddball of instant interest. But we're talking safe options here. It's OK to stand out, but it's safer to stand out *inside* the tribe, if you see what I mean.

This entails wearing an acceptable look (jeans, cargo pants, whatever) but tailoring it slightly to add a touch of individuality.

Dating

Avoid the trap of trying too hard every time. Similarly, guard against an inclination to stop trying altogether. Men get very wary indeed if a woman's dress sense starts to drop off, as they fear the advent of Lycra leggings. They will notice things that match, especially underwear. Non-matching says non-bothering. Big knickers scare them witless, and we all know they are unhappy about tights. If you want to ditch a man, undress wearing big knickers and pop-sox. No amount of explaining how they effect a better line under your clothes will work.

Women aren't as unkeen about little knickers as they try to make out. Boxers were only ever sexy when they were worn by Nick Kamen in that jeans ad. G-strings tell of mullet haircuts, but can be OK once you're established in a relationship. White or black short, tightish pants are probably safest.

Dating gives you a chance to present other facets of your incredibly complex and intriguing personality through your wardrobe, but fit clothes to occasion every time. And when in doubt, use mirroring. Wear clothes that are similar in style to your partner's. Looking like a double act will imply spiritual bonding.

For Life

Dressing for life can be fun as long as you dress primarily to impress yourself and then to impress your partner. Thank God it is possible to do both at once without looking like a refugee from 'Reader's Wives'.

When you stop taking an interest in yourself you cease taking an interest in your relationship. Forget all the old rubbish about figures automatically flabbing out and wardrobes becoming a style-free zone when you get older. You are in control of this in exactly the same way as you have been in control of it throughout your youth. Think ahead before you lose your grip. Even if your current partner likes you whatever your shape or style, think what will happen if you split up. How will you look when you get out there and start dating again?

Age is no barrier to looking good, and expectations have changed. You will need to be a lean, mean, stylish fighting machine for longer as marriages get shorter.

Long-term Style Mistakes

Dressing like the kids
Women who get sprigged up in floating floral frocks and men who get kitted out like one of the Famous Five need to realise they look something way beyond idiotic. These clothes are the utter antithesis of cool and sexy. I have seen adults wearing Alice bands and kiddie sandals and men carrying school satchels. And every time they have one or a selection of mini-me's in tow. Dressing like your children is neither cute nor funny. Stop it now.

Dressing like a slob
We all know it's nice to be comfortable. But there are some clothes that should never see the light of day again. These include any garments kept just 'for cleaning' or for 'doing the garden'. These have usually been dragged out of the bin, where a disgusted partner has placed them. There are enough good-looking casual clothes on this planet for you never to have to wear anything stained, grubby and ill fitting ever again.

Dressing old

I don't believe that mutton dressing as lamb is a sartorial crime, but I do believe that mutton dressed as much older mutton is. Dread the day when your partner comes home with a pair of cords with elastic waist inserts, or orders anything from that 'bland and comfy' catalogue that fell out of the Sunday papers. Somewhere out there is a world of combed cotton and tweed, rugby shirts and deck shoes and sports/casual, and I never want to join it.

Dressing to feature negative body parts

There are enough shapes and styles around to flatter any body form, so why dress in a way that exposes the worst bits?

Colour Psychology

The shade you choose to wear can say a great deal about you. For example:

- NAVY/GREY – professional, sensible, businesslike.

- BLACK – multi-faceted: fashionable, guarded, dour, stylish, mysterious, businesslike, aggressive.

- RED – the colour of sex, emotion, love and passion. Warm and extrovert. But also aggressive. Be careful, though. This colour is also understood by men on the dating circuit to say 'desperate' as well. Unsubtle at times.

- GREEN – folksy, in touch with nature, non-aggressive, empathetic, calm. Jade or emerald will have more bite.

- BROWN – low-key, low-impact. Can look depressed. Earthy. Dour.

- PINK – fun, funny. Baby pink will look passive and childlike, bright pink gives hints of instability and a strong desire to stand out.

- BLUE – the safe option. Usually flattering. Calm. Focused. Tasteful. Not too dull.

- BEIGE – dull. Rather low self-esteem. Dreary. Only wear this as a tasteful option if your colouring and personality tend to be wild and you want to tone down. If you are pale and boring, avoid it like the plague.

- CREAM – more vibrant. A high-energy pale colour.

- WHITE – a white shirt or T-shirt on a man is a high attractor. A white suit is as low as you can get, unless you're Gareth Gates. White on a woman hints at purity and weddings.

- PURPLE/MAUVE – strong and controversial. Artistic.

- YELLOW – optimistic, creative. High-energy.

Fabrics

All the 'natural fabrics', such as cotton, silk, denim, wool, leather and linen, are good. Avoid anything too structured and stiff; opt instead for something with movement and drape that is low-maintenance to wear. Garments should look comfortable and tactile, not awkward and scratchy. Check how you move in your outfit. Does it move with you? Can you sit, stand and walk easily in it? Do the shoes allow you to walk well or do you have to adapt to them?

For women

- Try to avoid anything too obvious, like satin or lace. Also watch out for the folksy, homespun charm of the small-print florals. What you might view as winsome and romantic most men see as frumpy and schoolteacherish.

- Cardigans can cause the same allergic reaction, as can tweeds.

- Avoid anything over-fussy, such as too many colours or patterns or too much jewellery.

- Brooches are ghastly. Get rid of them.

- Ditto shawls and pashminas. Men think they make you look like a granny.

- If you're wearing something clingy, don't just see how you look posing in it. Eat a large meal that includes baked beans and then slump a bit when you stand in front of the mirror. Does it still look good?

- Make sure no underwear lines show through.

- Don't wear memorabilia jewellery, such as rings, love-hearts and ankle bracelets that have very obviously been bought for you by a past lover. This is a bit like finding an ex's name tattooed on your man's body.

- Play up your best body feature and tone everything else down to draw attention to it. Emphasise too many good points and you could achieve over-kill.

- Most men prefer heels to trainers.

- Most men also prefer light make-up.

- Beware the 'instant attractor' trap. Too obvious usually doesn't work. One man I met who had done the dating agency circuit said he was bone weary of women turning up dressed in tight red dresses with bright red lipstick, trying to look sexy. Try for subtle – but not dull – instead.

For men

- Avoid anything flash or overtly sexy. Most women find this funny.

- Look as though you've made an effort but not spent hours in front of the mirror.

- When in doubt, clean jeans and a nice white T-shirt will always do unless you're going somewhere posh.

- Don't look more cautious than the woman. Turning up clutching a brolly and raincoat can look wimp-like.

- If you own a suit, never try to persuade yourself that you can wear the jacket and trousers separately, with something else. You can't.

- Avoid knitted jumpers in the early stages of a relationship.

- If you're wearing a shirt with your jeans, make sure it's a casual-cut shirt, not a suit-type one.

- Women are less impressed by designer-logo underpants than you think they are.

- Never wear funny socks.

- Or funny T-shirts.

- Never iron a crease in your jeans.

- Never reveal the toothbrush in your pocket, even if it's not the first date and even if you've already done it. It is seen as presumptuous.

- Try to look like the sort of guy who will buy fresh croissants and squeeze orange juice the next morning. Sexy-but-wholesome usually works.

- Check the contents of your pockets before she does. Jettison anything that suggests you had a life before you met her.

Dressing for Sex

Whether or not you dress to expose certain body parts depends on what you want to signal to a potential mate. Most people find sexy clothes more of a turn-on than nakedness, although revealing too much at once can make you look desperate rather than raunchy.

When we reveal body parts we reveal what are called items of body self-mimicry, the point being that certain parts of the body stand as clones or copies of other parts of the body.

The biggest sexual invitation a woman can give a man is to project her buttocks in his direction. This signal can be difficult to transmit once you have met, though, as humans normally stand face to face. This is why Kylie Minogue has cleaned up so effectively with her emphasis on the famous Minogue bottom. The gesture is far more suited to being sent generally rather than being specifically targeted, enabling Kylie to exaggerate it during her act on stage. Many other celebrities have started to mimic the look by sporting backless dresses to film premieres, giving them the opportunity to turn their backs on the cameras and reveal their bottoms along with the dress's main feature. Other women give buttock displays when they are dancing, or by wearing clothes that are tight-fitting around the bottom, emphasising its shape.

As most of our other sexual transactions are face to face the breasts have become popular clones of the buttocks, being pushed together and upward in cleverly cut bras to resemble the roundness of the buttocks more closely.

Midriff-baring is another fashion at the moment, with navel-piercing and navel displays increasingly popular. Often pop stars like Geri Halliwell will pose with arms raised as they display the belly. According to psychologists this gesture is erotic because it pulls the navel into a vertical slit, making it mimic the genital slit, which is why it is so popular in pin-up poses.

For men, the main genital mimic is the nose. Grow a bushy beard beneath it and the genital mimicry is complete. (Before you try this one at home, though, ponder for a moment whether you really want your face to resemble your genitalia so closely.)

Underwear

If you are dating an older man, keep in mind the wannabe aspect of sexual dressing for him. As old age beckons (which as far as they're concerned might occur from around the late thirties onward), men like to feel that they're not missing out. They like to think they have done it all at some time or another, and they start to brood about areas they didn't get to cover.

One of those areas will be sexy gear. Even it they're not sure they like this kind of kit, they think they should and they think they deserve it, which is massively important to them.

If a woman wants to know what stimulates and influences this kind of thinking, get your hands on a pile of lad's mags and porn. I am amazed at wives who dump their man's stash in the bin in disgust, or refuse to watch porno movies when they discover them at the back of the wardrobe, because they supply a piece of the jigsaw puzzle that might otherwise be missing.

Look through these mags and films. Keep in mind that this stuff could well be what your man was sexually reared on. He may even think this is somehow the norm. Look closely. Can you find one pair of tights or pop-sox? Are any of the women wearing Kickers or Organic sandals? Have any of them eschewed make-up on the grounds that they look unnatural in it? Do you see cardigans or big knickers?

No, what you see are thongs, suspender belts, stockings, black lace, stiletto heels and glossy lips. Learn something from this. High heels may be bad for your bunions but they remind men of sex. They make your legs look longer and more rigid. They also make you look more fragile, but at the same time aggressive.

Women, on the other hand, tend to be grateful if you remember to take your socks off in bed. We have fewer male sex-god role models, and those that we do have tend to go no farther than vests or bare chests. We'd like sex clothes on our men, but most of the really rude stuff on the market tends to be aimed at gay couples. We like the white outfit from *An Officer and a Gentleman* and we like firemen's kit, but try donning that casually in the bathroom before you hop into bed.

If you scoff at fashion you do so at your peril, because the clothes we choose to wear reveal much about our attitude to sex. The parallels are all there, and relatively unarguable. If you boast about your negative interest in the way you cover your body then it is fair to assume that your sexual techniques will be offhand, clumsy and lacking in flair or skill. It signals a complete lack of interest in your personal image, more likely to be due to depression than arrogance.

See your clothes as strenuous signallers, and keep this in mind throughout any long-term relationship. Sometimes it's all too easy to start dressing down in front of your partner without realising to what extent this signals the fact that you are taking him/her for granted.

CHAPTER THIRTEEN

Workplace Romances

Of course, people have always paired off in the workplace, but now it seems we're at it like never before. When I wrote my book *Sex at Work* I reported that around 40 per cent of people admitted to having met a partner at work, and I would estimate that number has risen since the book was published three years ago.

Why? Well, we still work long hours, which means less time to socialise, and most of us work harder, owing to increased workloads, globalisation, staff cutbacks and the fact that IT now enables us to do more. Many companies are merging and getting larger, and open-plan offices and business socialising mean people are more visible and more available. The increase in divorce rates has given rise to a new influx of older, born-again singletons on the market, and with most bars and clubs being aimed at young people the workplace is for some the only option for meeting a mate.

Companies have had to change their thinking to adapt to this date-fest. Where a workplace romance would once have been frowned on or even prohibited, these days bosses have little option but to, if not exactly encourage it, at least turn a blind eye.

E-mail has created a whole new way to flirt with a colleague, but it has also created a new double standard in body language behaviour. When we e-mail someone at work there is often a feeling of virtual reality, as though the message you are sending is going to someone other than the person sitting within view at another desk. People can send very romantic or raunchy e-mails but still keep their behaviour relatively formal when they encounter one another in the flesh – a characteristic of any written communication, even the electronic stuff.

The main problem with a workplace affair is that it can easily scupper your career, especially if you are sleeping with the boss. But don't let me put you off. The office can still be one of the best places at which to meet a partner. Many people keep this in mind when they select their career in the first place.

The Pluses

One of the good things about attracting a partner at work is that you don't have to be a 'one-hit wonder' in terms of your body language. Each day can be turned into your own little personal beauty parade for this colleague's benefit. You get to monitor their moods, attitudes, values and sexual attraction, and you display all those wonderful facets of your own.

Bodytalk advantages

- Your eyes get to meet across that crowded office many times per week.

- You can watch and monitor a potential mate more carefully that you could in public.

- You get to display yourself in action, which is 100 times better than just squatting on a bar stool.

- You get to bend, lean and stretch legitimately, thus displaying sexual body parts but without looking obvious.

- It is socially OK to smile your best smile without being accused of coming on to someone.

- You may even be allowed to touch (a handshake).

- You can use quite blatant flirt techniques (biting or sucking end of pen, smoothing or stroking hair, stretching and flexing chest muscles, eating cylindrical objects, like bananas, licking foam off top of cappuccino, etc.) without looking too comical or desperate.

- You can legitimately use more eye contact when speaking.

- You get more time to create a behavioural match, plus you get the platform on which to perform your own set pieces – assertive, brave, motivated, worried, nurturing, caring, strict, funny, etc.

- The resurgence of business socialising means you get to display your social skills.

- The upswing in stopovers (residential training courses, conferences, etc.) means opportunities to get drunk and play games together.

The downside

- Most people forget to look good at work, sitting slumped at their desk scratching spots rather than making an effort.

- If your flirting is too obvious you will alienate the rest of your colleagues, who will see your behaviour as devious and manipulative.

- Or you could be accused of harassment.

- Masking your feelings from colleagues if you receive a knockback and your pride is hurt can be difficult.

- As can performing a daily soap opera for their benefit if it does work out.

- Keeping an affair from your colleagues will be difficult. Your body language will give you away, so expect them to have guessed.

How to Hide an Affair

If you feel a workplace affair coming on, spend at least one whole day logging your normal body language towards the person you are becoming involved with. Make a note of how you greet them and how you look when you are speaking to them. Do not vary this in any way once the affair has started.

Keep an eye also on the way you react when colleagues mention this person. You may feel this stuff is obvious at this stage, but acting natural when their name is mentioned once you are in the throes of a hot and possibly illicit affair will be nigh on impossible, believe me. Even the mention of their name will make you look as guilty as hell.

Learn the skill of acting nonchalant. We all know the word, but few of us have ever had to act it. Even leading thespians struggle with it. Most are unable to muster anything more convincing than a raised eyebrow and a strange kind of head-wobble. Which brings me back to that piece of useless advice: 'just be yourself'. The problem is we don't know how we normally behave. It's something we just do, but never actually study. So make a study of it before it's too late.

The worst way to scotch rumours of an affair through your body language is to go into denial, acting as though the person you are intimate with is invisible to you during business hours. You avoid them and look away when they are near. Some people even go as far as being rude or sarcastic about the object of their lust. The complete lack of subtlety involved in this kind of visual and/or verbal denial will often be what first alerts colleagues to the fact that you're at it like stoats on Viagra.

If anything, flirt a bit with this person and show interest when they are around. This is the opposite of what your colleagues will be expecting – most couples stop flirting once they have started an affair. By continuing to do so you will have your colleagues confused, I promise.

Flirting at Work

Make the most of the formal/informal contrast that most office jobs provide. Dress smartly and look well groomed – something both sexes like, but which can look corny outside the workplace. Women may wear skirts and heels and men white shirts and jackets, all of which flatter the body.

Work will also provide an opportunity for formal interaction, and you should make the most of it, but without falling into the trap of 'power posturing' – trying to raise your status by means of your body language techniques. Power at work should be demonstrated by title or confidence, not childish displays that are a turn-off for everyone. The following are examples of power posturing:

- Finger-steepling

- Looking over the top of spectacles

- Leaning back in a chair with hands behind head and/or feet on desk

- Looking down your nose over a raised chin

- Sarcastic smiles

- Pretending to be busy when someone talks

- Signals of impatience, like tapping or walking away

- Placing both hands on hips

Create an effect that is polite and charming – the use of active listening signals combined with good posture and smart, formal gestures best achieves the formal/informal contrast. Occasionally introduce small informal acts, like the odd, knowing smile, warm glance or laugh, and you will have made yourself as irresistible as possible. One manager I worked with was extremely polite, businesslike and smart, but achieved a high-impact moment when he caught my eye and winked at me when a client was being difficult in a meeting.

The combination of highly civilised/sexual is a strong turn-on for many people if you get it right. It is why women like muscular men in uniform. Women can obtain a similar degree of enhanced attraction by wearing smart suits made of soft fabrics that cling, but without being too tight or too obvious. This achieves a look that most men would describe as sexy and classy. Skirts cut on the bias will do the trick, as will skirts that are not very short when you are standing but which rise to above knee level when you sit down. Check out skirts with a split, too. Evidently men find them sexier than a mini, even though most women find them just as obvious and corny. Choose one that you can control well, rather than one that parts up to navel level when you sit down at that important board meeting. Also watch out for skirts that split at the back.

Know exactly what you are showing and where.

Open-plan offices offer vast opportunities for long-distance walks, during which you get a chance to air the skills learnt earlier in the book. Carrying business paraphernalia can spoil the routine unless you hold it well. Bags and cases should be carried down by your side and should never make you look like a packhorse. Documents and clipboards need to be carried in one hand, and never across the chest like armour.

Non-sexual Flirting

Non-sexual flirt rituals are usually seen as productive in the workplace, where they can help overcome the awkwardness involved in daily proximity with virtual strangers, release tension between the sexes, and lighten the mood of a dull office.

Good flirts know how not to breach boundaries of good taste, and they know when to stop. They are alert to signals coming back at them and will discontinue the moment they spot signs that their behaviour could be inappropriate – an averted gaze, awkward body movements, nervous laughter, or a more formal tone.

Business flirting will usually cease when circumstances become more intimate – for example, if the two people involved have to work late alone, or share an individual office. Open-plan working provides the safest environment for workplace flirting, and such flirting has generally increased as a result.

'Good' workplace flirts will target anyone and everyone and employ their skills as a form of harmless soft soap or flattery. Women who target only men and men who target only women can make themselves unpopular with their own sex. Popular media figures tend to appeal in a mildly flirtatious non-sexual way to both sexes.

CHAPTER FOURTEEN

How to Be a Couple

Successful coupledom depends on synchronised choreography. Look at photos of couples in the newspapers and magazines. How can you tell the truly happy ones from those who are just playing to the camera? How can you tell when a friend's marriage is breaking down, even before he/she admits there is a problem?

Your ability to monitor your partner's body language and adjust your own to match it will be an essential skill throughout your relationship. If you start out of kilter you can still become synchronised with time and practice. But if you drift out of kilter and nothing is done about it you could find yourself heading for disaster.

Time and experience change the extent to which we are synchronised, along the following lines:

Stage 1
When you start a relationship you are still both separate entities. Embarrassment, nervousness or a desire to impress can make you clumsy. You don't know this person and so have trouble reading his/her mind. Because you have been told it's rude to stare you are trying to create some sort of match without monitoring closely.

Stage 2
You have agreed there is mutual attraction and so take yourselves away from your respective packs to meet up alone. This is a stage during which closer watching is appropriate, and so

you sit opposite one another, employing active eye and ear skills. You are beginning to tune in to the other person's moods, emotions and even sense of humour. You may be employing overt signals, like power displays, excessive nodding or laughing, in an effort to impress. This is the stage during which you begin to create empathy through mirroring.

Stage 3

Pre-sex, your frequency of touch – face and body touching, hand-holding, kissing – will increase, along with your warning signals to other men/women to keep their hands off. At some point you will begin to touch intimately – breasts, thighs or genitals – in a way that will move the relationship into the first stages of mating.

Stage 4

You are having sex, and so some of the body language tension between you has decreased. Your displays of sexual affection are now much more open and mutual. You touch all the time, and sit and stand with torsos pressed together. One of you may have developed superior leadership signals – having your hand or arm on top in any clench, and taking the lead when you walk. The other may well exhibit surrender signals in response, making him/herself look smaller and more fragile.

This is the period of extensive eye-to-eye gazing and face-checking to register approval and agreement. You have begun to mirror so extensively that you may even have begun to look and sound alike, copying gestures, facial expressions, behaviour displays and verbal tics.

Stage 5

You are now involved in long-term dating or cohabitation. The constant desire for sex has waned and your body language has begun to normalise and relax as a result. Cohabitation problems may arise early on, during the transition from stage 4 to stage 6, when a couple moves from being clones of each other, mistakenly believing that mutual sexual attraction automatically entails identical behaviour, to realising that cohabiting behaviour is a world away from this 'ideal'. This is when shock and irritation can set in over body language and behaviour differences that were not apparent during the dating stage. One partner may annoy the other by leaving the cap off the toothpaste or cutting their toenails in bed. The problem is not just one of etiquette involved – it's also the fact that such acts point up 'differences' where there are supposed to be none. And a stubborn determination to avoid reform is seen as a desire to create rifts in the body language togetherness.

Stage 6

This is longer-term cohabitation, during which we begin to lose the need to 'look' at our partner, just as we lose the need to look at ourselves to check understanding. Which means we lose the ability to tap into changes in thinking and behaviour. This is the era of assumption. The danger is that we have created an image and behavioural stereotype for our partner to create comfort and ease of transaction.

There is still some mirroring, but often friction, too, caused by increased diversity. Often the motivation to create a behaviour 'match' has decreased, owing to lack of energy or commitment or unresolved grievances. Patterns of negative match may have become commonplace, leading to serial arguments. When the two partners sit together in a pub or restaurant the conversation and non-verbal dialogue between them may be minimal. They may even sit looking in opposite directions. They may socialise separately. This need not be negative, though. A good sign is the couple arriving at an event touching or holding hands, mingling almost professionally but showing signs of mirroring even when they are on opposite sides of the room. The empathy and bond will still be there, even when distance is created.

Marriage MOT

There is no magic key to creating a good marriage. Some that appear lousy may last the course from wedding to funeral, while others burn brighter but snuff out sooner. It may seem irrational, but it is sensible to work out which of the two appeals to you most. Whichever it is, it is always worth considering your ability to monitor and adapt to change in your relationship. This doesn't mean a constant diet of Stepford wife-like submission, but an ability to duck and dive rather than falling into the trap of stereotype and assumption. There are times when we are all strangers to ourselves, so how can anyone else know us inside out? The danger with long-term relationships is that we are prepared to spend less time reading our partner's body language than we are the cat or the dog's.

Good sex requires constant eye and ear skills. In the initial stages you employ small body movements, like stretches, to show where and how you would like to be touched. The communication is simple. What you like or what you want more of you move towards. Your back arches and you push forward, or you relax. You respond by creating a mutual touch as reward. When you like something less you move back or turn away. All the time you are touching and exploring you will be keeping your eyes and ears open for signs of approval or disapproval.

In the initial stages you will work on a system of touch and check, whereby you touch or kiss and wait for a brief sign of approval or agreement to proceed. During the next stage you will be into touch and reward. It's the last stages which can get confusing. Intense passion can cause periods of silent tension. Go with the flow on this one. Most of the time it's a sign of mental and physical hunkering down for the big finale. Assume you're doing OK and carry on with business as usual. If the verbal soundtrack has stopped for a bit it's usually a good sign unless you start to hear snoring.

Be careful about the signals you create as a couple to insti-gate sex. What may seem cute or lovable in the early stages can irritate later on, even if nobody moves to change the script. Verbal dialogue that includes kiddie names or euphemistic body parts will age badly. In sensual terms they are about as seductive as sighing and then rolling on top of your partner. Hugs and strokes that lead to sex can also cause problems. Women often claim they would like a hug or a cuddle that doesn't always entail sex. For some reason this seems to confuse men. The result may be that a woman turns down a cuddle that she desires for its affection or emotional content in case it is a prelude to donning the Naughty Nurse kit once again.

One of the most attractive signals for initiating sex has got to be the one you started with – eye contact. Turning your partner to face you and looking deep into his or her eyes before kissing is romantic and sensual. If you face-touch or face-cup before you kiss you will consign you partner to *Gone with the Wind* heaven.

Think back to your dating days:

1. Turn to face your partner and use eye contact.
2. Get closer, moving the eyes down to the mouth, then back up to the eyes again.
3. Stroke the face or cup it in your hands.
4. Turn the head slightly, move faces slowly together, then kiss, lightly at first, then involving tongues.
5. Run one hand down your partner's back, then pull his/her pelvis close to yours (cue soundtrack of Enrique Iglesias and golden sunset).

If you have become rusty at this manoeuvre and fear rejection or even laughter, build up to it gradually. Remember what I said about the set pieces? Lighted candles around a Radox bath will only work if this is a regular feature of your relationship, otherwise it will appear too forced and slightly alarming. If the shine has paled for you, instigate small increases in touch and signal until you build up to this killer cocktail of eye contact and kiss.

One of the best methods of improving long-term body language is to revert to all those earlier signals of respect, interest, monitoring and checking that you used when you first fell in love. Look at your partner and notice what's new or different, or what has remained the same. Look when you are speaking to register response and when you are listening to read between the lines and understand the emotion behind the words.

Look for genuine smiles or laughs that start in the eyes before they move down to the mouth. Look for signs of stress or anxiety in repetitive or comfort gestures. Look for the denial gestures, such as the head shaking to register 'no' when the mouth is saying 'yes'. Check for signs of sadness or boredom in the eyes. Look at the posture. Is it slumped with negativity, or inflated with energy and positivity?

Watch how your partner's expression changes when he/she looks at you. This modification of facial expression will tell you all you need to know about the state of your relationship. If the features soften and the pupils dilate you can consider yourself loved. If the face remains impassive, or the expression is the same as when your partner speaks to other people, you should start to worry. If the face registers shared humour, through a suppressed smile and the eyes narrowing into an arc, you are probably friends as well as lovers. If the expression registers annoyance, irritation, boredom or social embarrassment, you may well be at the end of the relationship.

When Things Go Wrong

I once read a piece of advice that stated simply: 'If you think they are playing away then they probably are.' But the question will always present itself: Are my suspicions just a result of my own low self-esteem or paranoia?

Verbal quizzing is often the first route to clarification, but you then have several problems to contend with. It is easier to lie using words than through the non-verbal signals; you may be told what you want to hear, and believe it; you may still end up in conflict although you have little proof. Verbal sparring may result in a conviction on very little concrete evidence. The best speaker or the best liar wins.

But nobody can have an affair without consequent changes in their body language. Much better, then, to watch for any or all of the following body language and behavioural 'clues'.

First up, he starts buying new pants. This is easier to spot in an older guy as they often leave pants-purchasing to their wives. Some men have never bought a pair of pants in their entire lives, so furtive purchase of something other than those boxers printed with Star Wars characters should ring immediate alarm bells. Women are much more subtle. No middle-aged woman will suddenly arrive home clutching the Anne

Summers catalogue unless she is attempting to revive the interest of her current partner.

He/she closets him/herself away more at home. An affair creates a desire to spend time in your own space, mainly because the effort of concealment can be stressful. Being in love or lust requires long periods of quiet contemplation, and this is hard to achieve in front of a partner.

He/she will not liked being watched or followed.

Thanks to this new person in their life, he/she will start to acquire new body language gestures or expressions. Often they will be 'young' habits that sit uncomfortably on them. This is part of the mirroring phase, and one of the greatest give-aways.

There will be moments when he/she watches you in silence. Never mistake this for affection. They are sizing you up and making comparisons.

A man will act like a schoolkid with a new best friend. Watch for sarcastic laughs or eye-rolling when you speak. Everyone else bores them now, especially you. This is a hideous part of the growing process for them. You have become a species farther down the food chain.

I have mentioned how difficult it is for anyone to role-play 'nonchalant'. This skill will be called into play with increased frequency when he/she has an affair, and you can bet they will not be up to it. If you are combining gentle verbal questioning with a perceptive eye you will spot many bouts of fake nonchalance. Try lines like: 'So what does this new secretary of yours look like, then?' As he/she tells you they are rather plain and dull, watch for: lack of eye contact; the downturned mouth-shrug; the shoulder-shrug; the eyebrows raised in an expression of surprise and desperation; the eyes rolling up and to the right in an attempt to tap into the creative side of the brain. Any of these, and the true answer is that she/he looks like Pamela Anderson/Gareth Gates.

The facial expression to look for is the one that says your partner is surprised even to be asked. This is a kind of screen-saver expression which they will use when wanting to look casual. If it came complete with a caption it would read: 'Does she work as a lap-dancer? Oh, I don't know, really. Funny thing to ask.' The thought-bubble would read: 'Shit, she knows. Now how do I act nonchalant?'

You ask a question that would stop a tank in its tracks and he/she looks away to rearrange some flowers or dust a book, rather than gawping open-mouthed.

Common signs of lying are:

- Too much eye contact.

- Too little eye contact.

- Palms-up, shoulder-shrug gestures.

- All movement closes down.

- Face-touching.

- Nose-rubbing or mouth-covering.

- Eyes moving upward to his/her right when searching for an answer, implying creative thinking.

- Aggression (hit back hard to put someone off the scent).

- Overt astonishment ('How could you think I would do that ...!').

- Any tendency to use either more overt gestures or to keep more still than normal.

- Pretending to be asleep (you know when they're not).

- A sudden change in levels of affection, often an apparent change for the better, owing to guilt – more kisses, hugs and even presents (although it's always worth giving this one a trial run in case it's genuine reform behaviour).

Look for these common signs of guilt and stress:

- Shoulders raised higher, owing to muscle tension.

- Increased comfort gestures, like nail-biting.

- Increased gestures of impatience, like tapping.

- Increased blink rate.

- Increased swallowing or lip-licking.

- Increased sweating.

- Inability to sleep.

- Fast, staccato speech.

- Tendency to jump to ceiling height from prone position when the phone rings.

How to Hide an Affair

No moralising here, just a few tips to help you cover your tracks.

Again, make a study of your behaviour when you are acting normally with your partner. This logging of the status quo may save your life in years to come. If you play away you will need to replicate these everyday behaviours and gestures, and it will be very hard. That word 'nonchalance' comes into play again. Start work before the affair begins.

Pick a time when you are guilty of nothing, are not even contemplating anything, and imagine how you would react if your partner walked in and accused you of having an affair with a pole-dancer/male stripper. Would you act nonchalant? Certainly not. People only do this when they are as guilty as hell. You would stare. Your eyes would widen. Your mouth might drop open. You might even laugh. Practise all these and consign them to muscle memory.

Change nothing about your behaviour at home. Plan to be boring and annoying. Talk a lot about the really dull details of your job.

In addition:

- Act suspicious of your partner.

- Be a slightly bigger slob than usual; never over-groom.

- Don't change your hairstyle.

- Don't display weight loss.

- Don't start looking in mirrors more than usual.

- Don't change your perfume/aftershave.

- Don't start doing your own washing/dry cleaning if you haven't previously and do make sure you empty your pockets.

- Don't develop a new interest in *anything*.

Communication through Change

The bodytalk key to successful long-term relationships is the same as the key to building any relationship, whether within the family or in the workplace. I once asked the training manager of a leading fast-food outlet how they managed to empower their staff to create their positive customer care techniques, and was told that they were trained to do just one thing: look at the customers. When you are perceptive with other people – when you watch them and take time to monitor the signals they send out – you understand how to respond in such a way as to create a positive outcome. This needn't mean tailoring your every move and action to be pleasing to that person, but by being more aware you will have more control over the outcome of each transaction with them.

By ceasing to look at your partner you stop understanding him/her. When you stop looking you start working on assumptions. People change, along with their tastes, dreams and desires. Communication through change is vital, but most of us are uncomfortable making such communication verbal. For true insight, then, make sure you keep monitoring and understanding the non-verbal messages.

Afterword: Develop and Change

The key to successful sex and relationships, then, is your ability to adapt and change. Your bodytalk and behaviour skills are based on learned behaviours that received some kind of reward in the past, but that doesn't mean to say the reward will still be there in the future. We acquire habits and mannerisms that receive a negative response, but still we rarely make time for self-analysis or rehearsal of change.

If you want to create positive body language signals that will get a better reaction, your best ally is a full-length mirror. Practise on yourself first. Act out situations such as making an entrance, meeting someone new in a bar or club, or chatting to someone at a dinner party, and enjoy the fun of the role-play. After all, you learnt through play as a child. Remember pretending to be other people when you were young? This is a natural part of body language education and learning, so don't stop just because you have got older.

Rehearsal is vital. Watch people who you think do good body language, whether on TV or in real life, and then act out some of their gestures or expressions.

Learn how to create symmetry with your partner. Balance your body language to match his or hers. In many ways this will help your partner to do the same. In the end you should be as synchronised as ballroom dancers, your movements matching, through what will almost feel like a psychic link but will in reality be nothing much more magical than awareness and anticipation.

And don't forget to use 'eye listening'. Watch your partner to truly understand his/her thinking. Again: never assume – read all the time. Notice fluctuations in mood and desire. And through these skills learn how to create a lifetime of rapport and sexual charisma.

Index

BODYTALK AT WORK
How to use effective body language to boost your career
Judi James

What you *do* has as much impact as what you *say*. If you
want to succeed in business, your body language – your
appearance and mannerisms – must give out the right
message. And knowing how to interpret the signals of others
is an equally vital factor for success. In this fascinating and
information-packed book, presentation skills expert Judi
James shows you exactly how to improve your body language
and reap the benefits.

Discover how to:
- Create an excellent first impression
- Read and evaluate gestures, posture and other non-verbal
  signals
- Improve your communication skills
- Detect when people are giving you false or misleading
  information
- Assess your unique selling points and market yourself
  effectively
- Lead, manage and delegate successfully

MORE TIME, LESS STRESS
How to create two extra hours every day
Judi James

Do you wish you could create an extra two hours every day?
Do you long to be able to make your life calmer, more
ordered and under your own control?

In *More Time, Less Stress* business consultant Judi James shows
you that effective time management isn't an impossible
dream. She reveals strategies to help you beat the time
bandits and organise your life in a way that works for you.

You will discover how to:

- Use top time-saving tips you can put into practice
  immmediately
- Handle time-wasting stress and negative emotions
- Make decisions more quickly
- Prioritise your goals
- Organise your workspace and make technology work for
  you
- Apply 'time management' skills to your home and family
  life

If you enjoyed reading this book, you may be interested in the following Piatkus titles:

The Art of Sexual Magic
Margot Anand

Barefoot Doctor Handbook for Modern Lovers: A spiritual guide to truly rude and amazing love and sex
Barefoot Doctor

Becoming Orgasmic: A sexual and personal growth programme for women
Julia R. Heiman and Joseph LoPiccolo

The Big O: How to have them, give them, and keep them coming
Lou Paget

A Complete Guide to Love and Sex
Cassandra Eason

Creating Love
John Bradshaw

Dare to Connect
Dr Susan Jeffers

Hot Monogamy
Dr Patricia Love and Jo Robinson

How to Be a Great Lover
Lou Paget

How to Give Her Absolute Pleasure: Totally explicit techniques every woman wants her man to know
Lou Paget

If I'm So Wonderful, Why Am I Still Single?
Susan Page

If We're So in Love, Why Aren't We Happy?
Susan Page

The Lazy Girl's Guide to Good Sex
Anita Naik

The Love Laws: 9 essential secrets for lasting, loving partnership
Steven Carter

Make Love Work for You
Anne Nicholls

What Men Want: Three single professional men reveal what it takes to make a man yours
Gertsman, Pizzo and Seldes

Women and Desire
Polly Young-Eisendrath